I AM EVIDENCE

NOT A COINCIDENCE OF GOD'S LOVE

YOLANDA K. STITH

I am Evidence:
Not a Coincidence of God's Love

Copyright © 2023 by Yolanda K. Stith

All rights reserved. This book or any portion thereof may not be reproduced or used in any manner whatsoever without the express written permission of the publisher except for the use of brief quotations in a book review.

All biblical references are used from the New International Version (NIV) and the English Standard Version (ESV) ©.

Publishing Services provided by Paper Raven Books LLC

Printed in the United States of America

First Printing, 2023

Paperback ISBN: 979-8-9856737-0-8
Hardback ISBN: 979-8-9856737-1-5

First, I would like to dedicate I am Evidence: Not a Coincidence of God's Love *to the loving memory of my mother, Rosa M. Stevens, and my father.*

Second, this book is dedicated to my husband, Thomas A. Stith III, and our three amazing daughters: Kara, Kiah, and Kira! Thank you for your unwavering support and love.

Contents

Journaling 1
Assignments from God 3
    ೞ Pause and Reflect ೞ 7
Freedom 8
    ೞ Pause and Reflect ೞ 12
True Identity 13
    ೞ Pause and Reflect ೞ 16
Sense of Self 17
    ೞ Pause and Reflect ೞ 22
Purpose and Dedication 23
    ೞ Pause and Reflect ೞ 28
Perspective 29
    ೞ Pause and Reflect ೞ 33
Humility 34
    ೞ Pause and Reflect ೞ 45
Promises 47
    ೞ Pause and Reflect ೞ 52
Fulfillment 53
    ೞ Pause and Reflect ೞ 56
Knowledge and Fortitude 57
    ೞ Pause and Reflect ೞ 63
Faith With Intention 64
    ೞ Pause and Reflect ೞ 67

Forgiveness 68
    ख़ Pause and Reflect ख़. 72
Opportunity 73
    ख़ Pause and Reflect ख़. 78
Preparation 79
    ख़ Pause and Reflect ख़. 84
Personal Success 85
    ख़ Pause and Reflect ख़. 92
The Light 93
    ख़ Pause and Reflect ख़. 97
God's Favor 98
    ख़ Pause and Reflect ख़. 101
Perfect Timing 102
    ख़ Pause and Reflect ख़. 107
Power 108
    ख़ Pause and Reflect ख़. 115
Conviction 116
    ख़ Pause and Reflect ख़. 119
Victory 120
    ख़ Pause and Reflect ख़. 122
Reflection 123

1
Journaling

Journaling has been one of the most powerful tools in my toolbox for as long as I can remember. While sources often boast benefits such as increased mood, better cognitive functioning, and reduced stress, journaling also provides an outlet for allowing one's most cherished thoughts to come to life.

This book is designed to help you reflect, work through personal situations, and ultimately curate a plan to enable you to move toward the best version of yourself. Perhaps, sometimes you may feel beaten down or defeated because you don't fit neatly in the manmade boxes of life. This book will offer opportunities to craft journal entries based on prompts that closely align with the chapter discussion. The journaling questions provide opportunities for you to reflect and uncover situations that may be preventing you from moving forward in your life. The questions will assist you in actively applying this reading to identify your unique stumbling blocks, allowing you an opportunity to create a plan to overcome them.

I encourage you to answer the questions at the end of each chapter before moving on to the next one to capture your initial thoughts versus waiting until you read the entire book.

Creating a plan chapter by chapter will allow you the opportunity to immediately move forward with the plan you develop while journaling. The ultimate goal is to face your life's roadblocks head on, so you can take control of the specific issues you uncover during the journaling process. This is the opportunity to embrace your true self and discard the stereotypical feelings of persecution and false narratives placed upon you by others who impose their opinions on your life.

Now, grab your journal and let the process begin!

2

Assignments from God

God places intentions in your heart for reasons often far greater than you can imagine. While achieving personal milestones, God gives you everything you need along the way to accomplish His assignments. I wrote this book over and over in my mind, but I hesitated to craft words on paper. My thoughts wandered the full gamut as I tried to talk myself out of fulfilling this God-given assignment.

You may ask: Why would you talk yourself out of this God-given task? Please understand. I wasn't actively avoiding the assignment He gave me; there were so many unanswered questions. These unanswered questions paralyzed my ability to move forward. Why was I led to write a book? Whose life would I impact with my story? Did I possess the skills necessary to bring this book to fruition? Most of all, why my story? Could I write about my life when it made me so vulnerable? Who would listen and understand the gravity of my life experiences? Whose life am I destined to change from the writing of my story?

I was born as the result of a forbidden love. The difference in my parents' skin color prevented them from outwardly acknowledging their love. Although evidently a biracial person to the eye, I hadn't openly discussed my heritage until writing this book.

You see, my identity wasn't really a secret. Everyone I ever met believed they knew my story based on my outward appearance. People even alluded to a privileged life. It's very easy to incorrectly assume facets of someone's life simply based on the way they look. Although interracial relationships were forbidden, in reality, the persecution of such relationships was a façade. Interracial relationships, both consensual and nonconsensual, have existed since the inception of America. This history provides a familiarity with the varied external attributes of biracial individuals.

I encountered individuals who suspected my biracial ethnicity because of my hair texture, hazel eyes, and olive hue of my complexion. Releasing this truth allows me the chance to help others—individuals who face many injustices because the color of their skin prohibits them from nicely fitting in any one group—along their journey. I acknowledge I am different, but God wouldn't have it any other way!

I know what it feels like to follow God's will for my life. All the chaos dissipates. The peace of God, which surpasses all understanding, is present not only for me to see and feel but also for all those surrounding me to experience.

However, I began to notice the peaceful life I worked hard to create started to feel a bit chaotic. The peace I worked hard to obtain began to feel compromised.

After searching my inner thoughts, I realized my avoidance of the assignment to write this book, as directed by God, caused this feeling of uneasiness. My personal peace was at stake. I had not been obedient to God's word; I had not made any progress toward writing this book. I was too busy trying to talk my way out of being the person to write this book. I tried to convince myself and God that I wasn't the person to deliver this message. The truth is I did not want to be the poster child for this topic.

Upon reflection, I realized I was uncomfortable with unpacking my journey as a biracial woman.

I prayed and thought about all the assignments God had previously given me, which allowed me to reflect on the times I trusted in Him. It gave me the opportunity to remember the trust He placed inside of me and the power He gave me to conquer, achieve, and grow. For every mountain He brought me over, God bestowed upon me all of the tools I needed along the path to cross that mountain. While He didn't give me all of them at once, He never called me to a task without giving me what I needed to complete it.

I simply needed to remind myself of *1 John 4:4*

"You, dear children, are from God and have overcome them, because the one who is in you is greater than the one who is in the world."

When I dove into my personal feelings and recalled the many experiences of my life, I realized how this act of operating outside of my comfort zone allowed me another opportunity to align with God's plan for my life. My faith was put to the test. I had to relinquish my need to control entirely to God.

I was finally able to overcome the self-imposed obstacles without many of the answers I sought while attending a weekend-long stock market class. The instructor told us at the end of the weekend that we had to tell someone our deepest secret or vulnerability to grow as a market operator, as well as all other areas of our lives. Releasing the secrets would set us free. This was an opportunity to move forward on a journey to become the best person God created for His glory. My instructor's challenge was not a mere coincidence. It was a nudge from God encouraging me to step out of my comfort zone to complete this assignment. This nudge allowed me to see beyond the sea of questions floating around in my mind. Finally, answers to my questions were no longer as important as writing this book.

While desiring to return to the peace I knew before God placed this assignment upon my heart, along with the desire to fulfill God's assignment, I sat down one late Sunday night in August 2019 and began writing this book. Writing this book created a full-circle moment for me. Moments of indecision collided with the desire to talk about my journey as a biracial individual in a world filled with racism and evolved into a work of art, displaying God's love for all of us. This journey allowed me to first and foremost love God and Jesus even more than I thought possible. Secondly, I developed a deeper love and understanding for myself and my family as well.

This book is written because of this love. It is written for the people whose lives this story will impact—for those who have felt no one could understand their plight. Writing this book allowed me to understand this is not about me, and, believe it or not, it isn't about you either. It is about God's love for us, and understanding His grace and mercy is sufficient! It allows us to overcome the daunting tasks and experiences of our lives!

Use my story as a source of encouragement to put you in a position for God to use you and the abilities and talents He places in you to carry out your God-given responsibilities. I give all honor, praise, and glory to my Lord and Savior Jesus Christ for bringing me this far, not because He had to, or because I deserve it, but because He died for our sins and was raised to life to make us right with God.

◈ Pause and Reflect ◈

Has your peace been disturbed? Are you experiencing chaos in your life? This is the first opportunity to grab your journal to answer some thought-provoking questions and search your innermost being to discover areas of healing and potential growth areas. The goal is to recall and reconcile hidden issues or feelings of inadequacy along with changes you would like to make about yourself or the way you approach situations in your life. Remember to keep your journal close by to answer the questions located at the end of each chapter.

1. Do you feel called to a different path in your life? What are you called to be or do?

2. Would this calling allow you to be your authentic self? What does that authentic self look like?

3. Would it allow you to set and meet your goals and flourish in life? Does this opportunity provide fulfillment to you as an individual? Do you feel worthy?

4. Are you actively running toward or away from your assignment? Why do you think that is?

5. Do you have any expectations of God as you walk along your journey? What expectations do you have of yourself in your journey?

3
Freedom

Trusting God's will for your life is where the unfolding of your journey begins. My story of trusting and believing began in 1964, on a blustery, cold Sunday evening in an eastern North Carolina town. A woman, the mother to seven children, hurriedly removed clothes from a clothesline before the darkness took over the day. She quickly completed her chores so she could watch a show she enjoyed on television. She had so much responsibility outside of herself that her time was not her own. It was unimaginable to think she could steal time away for television. However, she found excitement in watching wrestling, of all things. Who knows? Maybe she drew some of the internal strength she possessed from viewing the sport.

Running toward the house before the show started, she tripped and fell into an electric fence circling the yard to prevent animals from escaping. The woman was expecting a child, somewhere in between her fifth and sixth month, she'd say.

Falling onto the electric fence caused her to show early signs of labor. Later that evening, her water broke, and contractions began the next morning. She was rushed to the hospital and gave birth to a baby girl, who weighed three pounds and 1.5 ounces. She was told the baby would not live through the night.

This baby girl was biracial—a child conceived by the union of a white man and a black woman. In 1964, in eastern North Carolina, race relations weren't exactly amiable nor quickly progressing toward common ground. African Americans were still marginalized in this poor, rural town—the "country," as it was affectionately called—a place where the Ku Klux Klan made its existence known.

Neither this woman nor her child was a priority to anyone at that time in history. I'm almost certain some thought she wouldn't receive the care she needed, nor would her newborn eighth child receive the necessary care, because of the woman's, and baby's, skin color. It wasn't how things developed; God kept the baby and the woman safe.

God's protection was obvious, and His light was shown by the excellent care the staff provided for the woman and her child. A nurse even helped the woman give her daughter a name and encouraged the woman to visit her tiny baby in the nursery. The newborn was so small she fit in the palm of her mother's hand. The mother visited her baby as often as they allowed her in the nursery.

The woman was released from the hospital several days later. She was told her child wouldn't live much longer, yet they encouraged her to visit her baby as often as possible. She traveled to the hospital to visit her new baby every day for approximately three months; despite the initial prognosis given to her by the medical staff, she never gave up on her baby.

Each day, the baby's health improved. She grew stronger and stronger. The baby proved to be a fighter, and she was determined to live. After three months of caring for her other seven children at home and traveling to the hospital to be there for her newborn, to her surprise, the baby was strong enough to go home. She didn't have any of the necessities to bring the newborn home, but it didn't matter. She took her baby home, lined the top drawer of her chest of drawers with a baby blanket, and used it as the baby's bed. Deciding where the baby would sleep was the least of her worries. Despite encountering mockery and jeers for having a biracial child, my mother praised God when she was finally able to take me home. She didn't know it then, but God had plans for me.

Along my personal spiritual journey, I realized the greatness of God's favor throughout my entire life. God protected me then, and He continues to show me new mercies every day. He wants us to understand the power of faith. He shines His grace and mercy on our lives. God has a plan for you and me. This is where I came to know the truth of **Psalm 139:13-14**

"For you formed my inward parts; you knitted me together in my mother's womb. I praise you, for I am fearfully and wonderfully made. Wonderful are your works; my soul knows it very well."

Due to the racial climate during the time of my birth, there is no doubt in my mind that my conception was not coincidental. He created me for his perfect plan. I am evidence for all to see His love, grace, and mercy. It's amazing how God has brought me so far. The closer I grew to Christ, the more He began to reveal to me the plans for my life.

First, at a very early age, I learned I am an exception, and it is okay to be different. When you can realize and accept you are different, God can use you because you no longer pursue fitting in where others believe you belong. It requires boldness and fearlessness to walk in your difference.

I remembered being treated differently by my peers. I wasn't black enough to be accepted or treated as a black girl, nor was I white enough to be accepted or treated as a white girl. North Carolina adopted the "one drop rule" in 1923: individuals with mixed European and African ancestry were usually classified as either mulatto, black, or sometimes white, solely depending on their appearance. I learned I was custom-made! It didn't matter what the law dictated. God knew exactly what He was doing when He made me. He strategically placed me here for such a time as this. I was not a mistake.

My parents might have been surprised by my arrival, but my Father in heaven was not.

I know I was fearfully and wonderfully made, and so were you. God has a purpose for you and me. Accept the plan and path He has laid before you and begin the walk to your destiny!

༄ Pause and Reflect ༄

Will you seek your purpose, or will you sit idly by in your comfort zone, refusing to accept God's calling on your life? Take out your journal and reflect on the following questions.

1. What evidence can you currently see that God's protection and favor are in your life? What freedoms has His presence offered in your life as you pursue your goals and His plans?

2. Have you always known God was with you during difficult moments, or are you learning to uncover the presence of His protection?

3. Do you find comfort or reassurance when you know God walks this journey with you?

4. Do you believe God will continue to protect you as you walk in your calling?

4

True Identity

As a young child, I recognized my skin complexion was different from that of my siblings and my classmates. Outwardly, my complexion was lighter than my siblings, who had two black parents. Comparatively, I stood in stark contrast to them, but they didn't treat me any differently. They treated and loved me as the baby of the family. I loved them, and they never felt like half-siblings to me.

However, other individuals in my extended family would not let me forget that I was a biracial child. While some acted out of malicious intent, others were simply ignorant and didn't know any better. They didn't consider how their actions made me or my immediate family members feel. Recently, one of my sisters told me when she used to introduce me as her sister, she just explained upfront that I had a different dad and that he was white. This prevented them from asking questions and pondering the reasons for our differences.

I was constantly asked if I was black or white. My answer to that particular question evolved over time. "I'm whatever color you want me to be" became my go-to answer after tiring of explaining "what" I was to inquiring minds. The color of my skin held no importance to me because it didn't dictate who I was as a person. It didn't impact or change all of the wonderful attributes God placed inside of me. I am compassionate of others and their feelings, I seek to find goodness in all people, and I want to see all people reach the area of success they desire. I strive to be the best version of myself in all areas of my life—as a child, I helped my mom with chores at home and worked hard to be a good student. As an adult, I have aspired to be a God-fearing leader and mentor who encourages others to pursue growth opportunities. God has been a present help to me, creating opportunities to mold me and even teaching me how to endure the painful experiences because of the color of my skin.

One day after school, I vividly remember looking in the mirror and thinking, *I like what I see*. Forced to recognize and accept my differences, my life was on a trajectory of growth from the inside out. I learned to sympathize with all people, black and white, and observe the hurt both ethnicities cause one another.

The racial unrest was most definitely real during my childhood, and sadly, it continues as this book is being written. Seeking personal growth and God's plan does not mitigate the realities of others' unkindness. As a people, we must mature and look at our own faults. It is so easy to point the finger at someone else for your pain, your obstacles, your decisions, and your life's outcome. The art of accepting the choices we make allows us the opportunity to learn there are consequences for every decision we make. We can't control others, but we can control our thoughts and our actions and decide how we will make this world a better place. We must look outside of ourselves to understand how our actions affect others. This journey we call ours is not about us as individuals. It's about what we can do for God's glory.

Although some tried to make me feel less than others, I honestly never felt that way as I journeyed to where I am today. I grew to understand I was born when, where, and to whom I needed to be born, and I didn't need to pacify anyone with excuses for any of the parties involved.

My differences were powerful. God made me just the way he intended. I had everything inside of me—everything God wanted to place inside of me to impact the lives of others for Him.

Socially, it was taboo for a white man to love a black woman. This hate-filled bias prevented my parents and others like them from simply loving one another because of the color of their skin. Race-mixing (miscegenation) was banned, and attempts were made nationally to ban interracial marriages by amending the U.S. Constitution three times. The last and final attempt to ban interracial marriage in every state failed in 1928. In 1964, the U.S. Supreme Court unanimously ruled that laws banning interracial sex violated the Fourteenth Amendment to the U.S. Constitution. In 1967, three years after my birth, the U.S. Supreme Court unanimously overturned *Pace v. Alabama*, ruling that state bans on interracial marriage violated the Fourteenth Amendment of the U.S. Constitution in *Loving v. Virginia*. Interracial marriage became legal throughout the United States.

If people have issues with the way God made me, or you for that matter, I quickly give the issues back to them. I suggest you learn to do the same. Ultimately, those issues are theirs to resolve, not mine or yours. I simply pray for them and ask God to allow them to overcome the inadequacies they project onto others.

☙ Pause and Reflect ❧

Have you ever intentionally mistreated or caused harm to anyone? Has anyone mistreated or caused harm to you? If your self-reflection doesn't uncover any intentional mistreatment of others, then continue to trust God to put you exactly where He wants you to be—impacting the lives of others for His glory. Conversely, if your self-reflection identifies unintentional mistreatment of others, capture those situations here and come up with a plan of forgiveness. The plan can be for you alone to simply acknowledge how your actions offended someone, or it could include the person who was impacted by your actions. The good news is you decide how you will move forward. Consider the questions below to assist you with identifying unintentional mistreatment of others. You can also capture times when someone has mistreated you and create a plan to forgive them.

1. Have you ever intentionally mistreated someone, even if at the time you felt they deserved it?

2. Do you carry any burdens around with you for your unjust treatment of others? Do you wish to absolve yourself by offering an apology? What would you say?

3. Have you ever been mistreated based on your appearance, skin color, or other different character trait? Did this mistreatment make you question your identity or place in life?

4. How did your experiences shape who you are as a person? How did they impact how you treat others?

5. Describe some commonalities among people with differences—in an effort to find common ground and foster greater acceptance in society.

5

Sense of Self

Do not let others' imperfections ruin you or your calling to fulfill God's amazing plan for your life.

Individuals who judge others' intent prematurely because of their outward appearance must live in a very lonely place. God made each of us in His image. What happened to getting to know others and learning about their character, hopes, and dreams? Think about how many great people they have not allowed into their circle. Think about the great experiences and missed growth opportunities just because they only observed the outward being and formed an incorrect opinion of others without engaging in meaningful conversations to determine common goals and common ground.

The act of loving and accepting others was lost when people became so self-absorbed with wanting to be better than their neighbors, instead of loving thy neighbor as yourself, as God tells us in His written word, ***Matthew 22:34-39***

> *"But when the Pharisees had heard that he had put the Sadducees to silence, they were gathered together. Then one of them, which was a lawyer, asked him a question, tempting him, and saying, 'Master, which is the great commandment in the law?' Jesus said unto him, 'Thou shalt love the Lord thy God with all thy heart, and with all thy soul, and with all*

thy mind. This is the first and great commandment. And the second is like unto it, thou shalt love thy neighbor as thyself.'"

My biological father was unable to spend a lot of time with me during his lifetime because of the obvious racial tensions. The occasional visit and phone calls are etched in my mind, and I feel like I can almost recall all of them. While he was unable to be with me for much of my life, looking back, I know my Father in Heaven was there with me every step of the way. There were so many strengths He placed in me at birth that were waiting to be realized. He also placed specific undeveloped strengths in me to discover as I walked along my journey. Each of us has these strengths, unique to whom He created us to be.

However, as a young child, I didn't know the strength God placed in me. I was painfully shy and only wanted to be with my mother. I found comfort in her love for me. I didn't want to spend time with the other children outside of my family because they were critical of my being. I didn't look like them. It is truly amazing how God kept me during those times. It is during this most difficult time that I began to realize the strengths God placed in me. I implore you to move forward in your known strengths and watch God reveal the additional strengths you possess as you move forward with that which He trusts you to do in this world.

I was not ashamed of the person God created in me. I was more ashamed of the prejudice shown toward me and others like me. In **Philippians 1:20-22** in the letter to the believers in Philippi, Paul states,

> *"I eagerly expect and hope that I will in no way be ashamed, but will have sufficient courage so that now as always Christ will be exalted in my body, whether by life or by death. For to me, to live is Christ and to die is gain. If I am to go on living in the body, this will mean fruitful labor for me. Yet what shall I choose? I do not know!"*

SENSE OF SELF

I chose to live in the body God gave me without shame.

He is the creator of all good and perfect gifts. Stand up and own your true sense of self created by Him. I am different, not defeated. God has a plan, and we are never alone. He is always with us. ***Philippians 1:6***

"Being confident of this, that he who began a good work in you will carry it on to completion until the day of Christ Jesus."

As for me, I chose to move beyond the prejudice and walk the path laid for me.

Along my journey, I met individuals who didn't seemed bothered about the color of my skin. They accepted me just the way I was. I could tell right away when I came into contact with those who accepted me and what I could offer as a person. I am so grateful for those individual angels God sent my way, along with those He will continue to bring into my life. God will send good people into your life as well, and they will serve as angels who will travel with you along this journey. Those individuals cheer you on to greatness. They aren't jealous of you or your achievements. Angels are anointed individuals sent to us by God to assist as needed. They will provide guidance, assist you in your growth, and even protect you as you seek to do the will of God.

Initially, I was unaccepting of anyone appearing to help me. I learned to rely on my own capabilities and myself in every area of my life. This proverbial box I built for myself became a lonely and limiting place. The lonely part requires no explaining; I'm sure you experienced loneliness in some form or another, either at your own doing or because you were not included. I became very efficient at placing a limit on the number of people I allowed to enter my inner circle. I was very guarded about the individual thoughts, people, and perspectives of others that I allowed to become a part of who I was as an individual. I sought out the motives of people, their thoughts, and ideas before I allowed them into my life.

Being judged because of my biracial identity created a breeding ground of distrust of others. Through trial and error, I learned how to discern if people had good or bad intentions when they came into my life. Self-reliance became my mantra. I developed a sixth sense and trusted it before allowing anyone—I mean anyone, adults or children—to get close to me. There were teachers who dished out their fair share of racist acts. I was keenly aware of those who accepted my differences and those who didn't. My sixth-grade teacher was very supportive of me. She wrote me a letter expressing the joy I had given her as a student. She told me I could become anything I wanted to be in life. She expressed concern that I would come across a boy who would try to take advantage of me because I was a very attractive young lady. She advised me not to get caught in the web of the wrong crowd, namely the do-nothing crowd, the trouble crowd, or any other crowd with no future.

My sixth-grade teacher and the letter meant the world to me. I often used the words in her letter as inspiration to help me overcome some of the most difficult times in my life. The words of encouragement served as a source of strength for me, especially when others tried to intimidate me or make me believe I wasn't enough.

I still have the letter she wrote me all those years ago. She was an angel sent to me by God. He knew I needed her positive influence in my life. He knew I needed someone other than my mother when I needed guidance. She was a woman of strength, courage, and tenacity. She modeled those virtues, and she wore them well.

Ultimately, I was able to determine who in my life intended to help or hurt me. Some people are meant to be in your life to help you if you are open to accepting them. Accept those God-given angels and their assistance when God sends them to help you navigate your calling. ***Psalm 91:11***

"For He will command his angels concerning you to guard you in all your ways."

God's unconditional love, as proven through his gift of our Lord and Savior Jesus Christ, helps us to accept the other gifts He sends us to complete the tasks of our specific journey.

☙ Pause and Reflect ☙

Will you recognize those angels sent from God to walk along your journey to aid you, or has the burden of others' perception weighed you down so much that you are unable to see them? As you ponder the answers to these questions, begin praying, and ask God to provide clear directions as you consider the path set before you. You should also pray specifically for the people who surrounded you during times of decision and indecision and request clarity about them in your life. Reflect as you answer the following questions and include any other thoughts that came to your mind as you were reading the chapter.

1. Will you allow others to tell you your differences prevent you from becoming the person you were called to be for God's glory?

2. Will you allow others and/or your own self-sabotage to keep you from reaching your calling? If yes, ask yourself why.

3. Who are the people who accept you as you are?

4. Who are the people who don't accept you?

5. Are you constantly trying to fit in with those who don't accept you? If yes, why?

6. What do you hope to gain or achieve from seeking acceptance from others?

6
Purpose and Dedication

When God created us, He knew why He created each one of us—our ultimate purpose. He gave us the talents, appearance, and heart to accomplish the tasks He intended for us on this earth. Writing this book gave me the opportunity to look back and know without a shadow of a doubt that the favor of God has always been in my life. He has been, and continues to be, with me every step of the way. Arriving at this point of realization was not easy for me, but I refused to give up. Anything worth having or achieving will not be easy. Put your faith and trust in the Lord, and watch Him work it out for your benefit.

Deuteronomy 31:6

"Be strong and courageous. Do not be afraid or terrified because of them, for the Lord your God goes with you; He will never leave you nor forsake you."

God's word is so true! I am a living witness. There are so many things that *could* have gone wrong, that others *wanted* to go wrong, and that *did* go wrong in my life. *But* God kept me, and He never left me throughout it all.

I have had my share of accomplishments and my share of disappointments. Even though I was the youngest of eight children, I often felt like the oldest child. Maybe it felt this way because I was one of the last two children left at home with my mother. My other siblings moved on with their lives and built families of their own. As I stated earlier, my mother was where I found security, comfort, and love. It was the unconditional motherly love that she nurtured me in, regardless of the pain she experienced because of life's circumstances.

God allowed me to receive the love I needed to become secure within myself. I am so grateful for the woman He gave to love me. She was selfless in everything she did, never placing her own needs before her children. She taught me everything she could while also letting me stretch beyond her growth. While my mother was educated, there came a time when I was more educated than she had become due to the restrictions life placed upon her, a mother to eight children with the thought of their wellbeing more important than even her own desire to achieve beyond the schooling she had received. By the age of 10, she began to prepare and teach me the things she knew. I completed applications and deposit slips, wrote checks for her signature, and went with my mother to the bank and grocery store to assist in handling her business. She taught me how to cook, clean, wash and dry laundry, and iron clothes. She often talked about being in a position to take care of myself.

All this time, God was grooming and preparing me at a young age, and I didn't even have a clue. ***Ephesians 2:10***

> ***"For we are God's handiwork, created in Christ Jesus to do good works, which God prepared in advance for us to do."***

God will never leave you, nor forsake you.

As I prepared to graduate from high school, I knew I wanted to attend college. My mother also wanted me to study at a university because she felt additional schooling was a path to success. My siblings had chosen different paths so there wasn't a template for me to follow. How would I make this a reality? Neither of us knew the process for college admissions. I remember both of us attending a meeting held at

PURPOSE AND DEDICATION

my high school where they discussed the college application process. She left it all up to me to figure out, and with God's grace, I navigated the college admittance process. I became the first and only child in my family to attend a university and receive a bachelor's degree.

The summer before my freshman year of college, I worked two jobs. During the day, I worked eight hours from 7:30 a.m. until 4:30 p.m. in an office setting, assisting customers. In the evening, I worked at a local high school, cleaning classrooms after summer school, emptying trash, and sweeping floors from 5:30 p.m. until 9:00 p.m. to save money for college expenses.

I was exhausted from working all day, and I only had enough energy left to sleep until the next day began. I repeated this five days a week during the entire summer. I lost several friends because they just didn't understand why I was exhausted on the weekends. They didn't understand why I didn't want to use my weekends to go out and party with them. I wanted to rest, and more than that, I wanted to accomplish more than my family had before me. I wanted success!

At 18 years old, I didn't know what success was. I only knew it was different from my experiences as a child of eight siblings. I realized everything I wanted was possible through hard work and perseverance. I worked my way through college to obtain the financial means needed to achieve my goals. During those moments, I was oblivious to the character development taking place inside me. I refused to give up on my commitments. My young adult years were some of the most challenging of my life. I learned that the decisions I made always had consequences. I intended to remain focused and make the best decisions for me. I made mistakes along the way, and in those mistakes, most of my learning occurred. Staying focused and moving forward is where I found strength.

I vividly remember thinking not only was I different on the outside, but I was different on the inside as well. God instilled this "no quit" mentality inside of me. While everyone attended football games, basketball games, and parties, I worked, studied, or attended classes. Just like in high school, some students judged me because of my appearance and because I decided to approach issues I faced differently.

College was everything I had heard it could be and more. Just like any other young adult, I happily explored my independence outside of my family's shadow. College was a time to prove to myself that I could become successful. The necessity to work while attending college afforded me the opportunity to interact with many people from various backgrounds and socioeconomic classes. I worked with other college students, single parents, and those already with spouses and children. I also met a lot of different people when I worked for a local credit union. I learned so much about myself in that position. I am an extrovert. I am not shy at all. I discovered my interest in assisting others with issues and solving problems. I found I was happiest when helping others.

Moments of confusion or sadness mostly centered around the actions of others. Sometimes, coworkers competed for the attention of the supervisor or manager. I experienced the uncomfortable situation of coworkers who didn't want me to advance in my career. Regardless of the challenges I faced, I refused to quit. **Galatians 6:9**

> *"Let us not become weary in doing good, for in proper time we will reap a harvest if we do not give up."*

Many times along my journey, I thought it would be easier to give up and give in, but God wouldn't let me quit.

Working while being a college student was one of the most difficult phases of my life, but, unexpectedly, it allowed me to develop character and the perseverance to see all things through to the end. It created a strong work ethic that strengthened this "no quit" clause inside of me and fueled my determination to succeed in every area of my life. I met and worked with some great people during those years. I observed them and mirrored the qualities of these individuals to become a successful professional.

While in college, my favorite uncle, my mother's youngest brother, and his now ex-wife were my God-sent angels as I left home for the very first time in my life. They didn't coddle me and allowed me to grow as an individual, but they were there if I needed them. I appreciated having their support as I advanced through college.

I met my husband, Thomas, in college, and he became one of the angels God put into my life. He always supported me in my pursuits. He accepted me for who I was as a person. He saw my raw potential, nourished my development, and continues to support me in every area of my life.

My accomplishments serve as the foundation upon which I currently stand. You will and probably already have faced several challenges in your life. Maybe the outcome of those challenges was not as promising as you originally thought. Just keep moving forward. Listen to God's voice telling you to keep moving. He never said it would be easy. Instead, think of the testimony He is preparing for you to share with others to glorify His name. ***1 Peter 5:10***

"And the God of all grace, who called you to His eternal glory in Christ, after you have suffered a little while, will Himself restore you and make you strong, firm, and steadfast."

Understand, beloved, you are not an accident or coincidence. God created you to endure the obstacles set before you to make you stronger and give you a testimony to share with others. God wants you to talk about the good news of His Glory and to share how He brought you out of those situations you felt you were unequipped to accomplish. During these times, God is closer to you. One of my sisters reminds me about God's goodness when she affectionately says, "God didn't bring you this far to drop you!"

The current challenges in your life do not determine the outcome of your future. Self-acceptance will help you achieve a purpose you never imagined. God is preparing you for greater!

☙ Pause and Reflect ❧

Do you know what your life's purpose is? Are you happy when you find yourself dedicated to making a difference in someone's life? Is there a specific area where someone compliments your actions? Many times, God provides a glimpse of our life's purpose in the areas where we are simply just helping someone to move forward. However, the inability to receive those nuggets of insight are common. Often times, being dedicated to specific tasks prevents us from seeing the other areas of strength because we can do them with poise and ease. While pondering the questions below, consider those strengths which come so naturally to you that they are seamless in effort. This may be where your natural abilities will serve a greater purpose.

1. Was there a time when you accomplished tasks you didn't think you could achieve? Do you believe you accomplished them on your own?

2. Do you recognize God's intervention on your behalf?

3. Was there a time that you felt like giving up? Did you?

4. Was there a time you felt like giving up, but you didn't?

5. What tasks or functions give your life purpose? Which ones are you most drawn to? Are any in the service of others or in service of God?

7

Perspective

We all are familiar with the phrase "there are two sides to every story" as it relates to one's view of any situation. Let me share with you the story of how I met my husband, and then how my husband met me.

Hers…

As a college student, I still enjoyed the comfort of the relationship I shared with my mother. I knew she wanted the best for me, and I could count on her unwavering love and support. When classes were over and the weekend came, I always wanted to return home to soak in the rejuvenation she provided for the week ahead.

At my alma mater, the awards ceremony was held during the spring semester. That particular semester, it was held on a Friday afternoon, and I committed to attending the ceremony with a couple of my friends. After final classes, we met at the gymnasium where all of the university's large events took place. However, just like all the weekends before, I planned to travel home for the weekend. I couldn't wait for the ceremony to end. Finally, the last speaker gave their presentation, and we hurriedly exited the gymnasium to walk toward the car. Out of nowhere, a very attractive young man dressed in a suit approached the three of us, introduced himself, and invited all three of us to eat at a local restaurant.

I needed to leave or endure the after-work traffic on the highway. We didn't know him, so we politely said no and began our walk to the car. However, he followed us. It turned out he and his colleague were parked near our car. He approached us again and asked to speak with me. He gave me his business card, and I shared my contact information as well. Usually, I gave a fake name and telephone number to any man who showed interest in me. I did not want to pursue a relationship because of a painful prior relationship.

After that day, there were several unsuccessful attempts for us to meet one another again. I had already decided he was involved with someone or dating several women. Let's be real: he was attractive, intelligent, and an established professional. He had to be involved with another female. Our schedules didn't align, so we were unable to meet in person. I went on with my normal routine.

However, he made an effort to stay in touch via phone calls. We eventually met one day very briefly at the library, where I studied for exams and finished a research paper. He was leaving the state to travel for his job, followed by a personal trip, for several days. He wanted the two of us to meet again.

Finally, our schedules aligned, and we went to dinner together after he returned from his travels. The time we shared proved to be easy and enjoyable. It was as if we had known each other all of our lives. The two of us shared our backgrounds, goals, and dreams. We even talked about my upcoming exams. I was unable to accept any of the other invitations he extended to me as I prepared for finals. However, he always made an effort to call me to see how I was doing. I was impressed with the concern he showed for me. This meant a lot to me and allowed me the opportunity to see the goodness of his heart. He extended the kindest gesture I had received from anyone in a long time. The day before my exams, he sent me a dozen long-stemmed roses with an encouraging note to do well.

Once finals were over, I needed to pack and move back home for the summer. He helped me pack my car with my belongings. We stayed in touch over summer break, fostering the beginning of a lasting friendship. He eventually visited me at home and met my mother.

PERSPECTIVE

This is my side of the story, and I'm sticking to it!

His…

Thomas eagerly anticipated the Spring Awards Ceremony. Our alma mater prepared him to pursue "excellence without excuse." Receiving an invitation to attend the awards ceremony as a special guest of the university was indeed an honor. While he served as Special Assistant to the Governor in his professional capacity, his attendance was a source of pride because his education and preparation during his college years helped form the foundation for him to excel. He wanted to give thanks for the role the university played in his life. He had no idea that his prayers of many months were about to be answered.

His relationship with God had matured since his younger years, and with that maturity came the understanding of the importance of finding a woman with whom he could share his life. Was he perfect? No. Was he striving to let God lead his life? YES.

His prayer was very specific: "Lord, please bring a woman to share in my life with a loving heart, without experiences that will damage our relationship, and for us to love one another for the people you made us to be." This was a constant prayer in his mind.

However, he had no idea God was about to answer him in a university gym! There were thousands of people in the basketball gym. He and his colleague sat in the VIP section near the stage surrounded by hundreds of students and guests. After sitting down, he began to look around at the large crowd around him. Almost immediately, he noticed a beautiful young lady in the upper-left section of the gym. Her smile said it all. It was her! He knew in his spirit that he had to talk to me. God answered his prayers, and he could not miss the opportunity to speak to me. You may say this was just a physical attraction. He says it was not. He knew in his spirit I was different. He has told this story many times, and most recently, he said it seemed that there was even a light around me that day. He said he felt like God said, "You wanted it to be clear. You prayed for her. Here she is!"

He stared at me during the entire ceremony, and in his mind, I stared back the entire time. He thought I smiled at him throughout the entire program.

The ceremony ended, and he quickly rose to his feet and told his colleague, "I have to find her." As hundreds of people filed out of the venue, he was concerned that he would not be able to find me. I exited from a staircase above him, and he came out from a different door. Every step along the sidewalk enhanced his anxiety that he would never see me again. As he walked up the sidewalk and the crowd thinned, he realized I was right in front of him and only a few steps ahead.

There I was, smiling and laughing with two other young ladies. He quickened his pace and caught up to us. Speaking to the entire group, he asked where we were going. He doesn't remember the answer because his attention was focused on me. He prayed, and God answered his prayers. He offered to take us to lunch, remembering his college days only a year or so earlier—the café was not known for the best food in Durham. We politely declined, and he wished us well. He says his heart fell to the ground.

I prepared to get in the car, and I heard a voice say, "May I speak to you a moment?" It was Thomas again. Thomas told his colleague at the end of the program about the young lady staring at him throughout the program and how he had to find her. His friend's encouragement gave him the confidence to try and develop a connection with me one last time. He gave me his contact information. I wrote my actual name and contact number on one of his business cards.

Over the next four years, our friendship grew into a relationship. It was during the fourth year of our relationship that we became engaged, and a year later, we married. God has since blessed us with three wonderful daughters and thirty-three years of marriage. Our three daughters are amazing young ladies who pursue their own paths for God's glory.

☙ Pause and Reflect ❧

Have you ever found yourself in a place where you don't see things the way others perceive them? In this chapter, you were introduced to two different perspectives of one single occasion: the meeting of two individuals. Think about the times when your perspective of an experience was different from those around you. How did your willingness to accept others' thoughts or ideas help or hinder your progress? Write about several of these situations where you were resolute in your feelings about the situation and weren't open to receiving or listening to a different perspective. Looking back, do you think there was value in the situation either for you or the individual who didn't take the time to listen to your perspective? Capture your thoughts in your journal and decide how you will move forward with knowing there is usually two perspectives in every situation.

1. Do you believe God placed someone unexpectedly in your life to help you along your journey? What do you think was their purpose? Did they help you?

2. Are you open to receiving the blessing of having others share your life with you?

3. Do you seek to be the best version of yourself? What do you do to better yourself?

4. Are you trusting and praying for God to send the individuals that will assist you during the next phase of your journey?

5. Was there a time in your life when you met someone and, at first, you didn't believe them to have a great impact on your life? Did they after some time? How so?

8

Humility

After graduating from college, I devoted my time to pursuing my first "real" career opportunity. I printed copies of my résumé and drove to several companies to inquire about job opportunities.

The very first building I entered, with fresh optimism, felt like the exact place I was supposed to work. I opened the big, heavy glass door and approached the tall reception desk. I noticed two people talking. I introduced myself and asked if they had any available employment opportunities. Immediately, the two people echoed the word "no."

Despite their answer, I inquired about the company and the type of industry it represented. I shared a bit about my work experience and thanked them for their time as I prepared to walk away. The gentleman asked me for a copy of my résumé and told me about a position that would become available in a few weeks for an office services clerk. He asked if I had any interest in the position. I said, "Yes!" He explained someone would call me within a couple of weeks with more details.

I left the building that afternoon knowing God had sent me to that specific building. I also returned home with overwhelming confidence in my future working for that company. I received a call two weeks later that led to several interviews with individuals from the company, including the person I met that first day. I discovered that the man who took my résumé was the HR Manager. After a month of interviews, I entered the doors as the new office services clerk.

Philippians 4:6-7

"Do not be anxious about anything, but in every situation, by prayer and petition, with thanksgiving, present your requests to God. And the peace of God, which transcends all understanding, will guard your hearts and your minds in Christ Jesus."

The job opportunity God provided for me after graduation was a prayer request I repeated for months. God knew I needed a full-time permanent job. He knew before I even asked. After all, He put the desire for success in my heart. God didn't give up on me because I didn't give up on Him. I kept moving forward, and He kept making a way for me.

Have you ever had the feeling that you are right where you are supposed to be? I have. I knew when I accepted the position. Many of my peers accepted higher-titled positions. After all, we had our degree; the world taught us to expect employment with a big title and most importantly a high salary.

When I accepted the position, none of that mattered to me. I knew my work ethic and God's grace would make a way for me. I only had to trust and believe His word, as I had done so many times before.

The moment I set foot in the office and was introduced to my coworkers, I knew instantly the position I aspired to within the company—that of a commercial underwriter. I had no idea how long it would take for me to progress to that position, and to tell you the truth, I wasn't concerned about the time. I just knew I would get there eventually. I arrived at work early and left late. I used all of the natural abilities God gave me to perform my job well.

My manager assigned me tasks to complete that I knew nothing about, but that didn't stop me. I conducted research, asked questions of my colleagues, and developed action plans to see the assignments through to completion. One day, about four months into my tenure, my manager called me into her office; this wasn't unusual as she often called me into her office several times a day to discuss developing issues. She asked if I had thought about any other role within the office.

I knew I wanted to become an underwriter, but I didn't know what to say. I didn't meet one of the criteria to apply for another opportunity within the company. I had only been there a few months. I really liked working for her, I liked my job, and I didn't want to offend her by appearing ungrateful for my current position. But I knew I could do more.

Without warning, I blurted, "I want to be an underwriter, but I know I must be in my current position for one year before I can apply for another one."

She looked at me with amazement and a half smile on her face. She expressed how it was a delight to work with me, and she noticed my work ethic in my current role. She and the vice president of our office recognized my dedication and tenacity as I pursued my job. She told me about an underwriter trainee position posted on the employment opportunities board—I was keenly aware of the posting.

Secretly, upon first glance of the posting, I felt great joy because the opportunity I silently prayed for on my very first day presented itself. A piece of the puzzle fell into place sooner than expected.

However, after reading the posting, my excitement dissipated. I didn't meet one of the requirements of the posting: I had not been with the company for a year. I quietly assured myself I would be prepared for the opportunity the next time and dismissed any other thoughts about the position. That is until my manager called me into her office.

She informed me that because of my work ethic and resolve to meet deadlines, our vice president permitted me to apply for the position. I was beyond excited, and I told her I would complete the application as soon as I finished the computer project she had previously assigned me.

She halfway laughed and said, "Complete it by tomorrow."

I finished the application knowing several others applied for the position. Colleagues with years of experience all discussed their desire to compete for the position. I submitted my entry and simply continued to perform my job as before.

All applicants went through an interview process, which took some time, but I didn't let it distract me. My mindset was that I knew what I wanted and would work to grow into that position, even if I wasn't chosen at this particular time.

Several weeks later, right before a holiday, the hiring manager called me into the conference room and told me that I was chosen for the position. I was asked to take the next day off because some long-time employees applied for the job, and HR wasn't sure of their response. I went into the long weekend amazed by my good fortune.

I cannot and will not tell you this happened because of me. Honestly, it happened because of God's grace and mercy on my life. He saw every struggle. He saw every tear. He knew my heart, and He knew my faith was in Him. **Romans 8:28**

> *"And we know that in all things God works for the good of those who love Him, who have been called according to His purpose."*

This scripture held true then, and it continues to hold true throughout my life.

Are you seeking a promotion? Are your abilities greater than the job requires? Are you humbly waiting for your next opportunity? Are you pressing toward your goals even when others try to hold you back? No matter what we endure and how difficult it may be, there is a reason we experience such challenging times. Keep your hand in God's hands. Never relinquish your faith to anyone or anything. The answers and inspiration you need are found in God's word, and peace comes from the personal relationship you develop with God and our Savior Jesus Christ.

The new position was mine, and there were a lot of components to learn! I welcomed and approached the opportunity the same way

I had all other areas in my life. The new class of trainees traveled to the company's corporate office in another state throughout the next year. The entire year of training allowed me to meet over 300 of my colleagues from different states who desired to learn and excel in the insurance industry.

During the first night of our training, we all gathered to have dinner together. I realized I was the only black person among the entire trainee group. I was amazed because God's favor on my life allowed me to be among a group of people expected to lead in their respective disciplines. As a class, we all bonded over the desire to become experts in the industry. Many of us became friends and kept in touch after our year of training was over. I really never felt as if I was judged because of the color of my skin among my peers. Eventually, we broke into our respective disciplines for more focused training. I was hired as an underwriting trainee. Thus, we focused on the underwriting process, company policy, guidelines, standards, and development of new business for the company.

This career shift presented me with new and exciting experiences: my first time flying, my first time traveling north, and my first time staying away from home for longer than a week. Traveling and learning to navigate my way around the airport gave me insight into my strengths. Financially, I was doing well. I enjoyed my job, and my coworkers were a great group of individuals. It also allowed me to improve on areas in which I struggled. My job stretched me mentally and emotionally.

After successfully completing the trainee program, I was promoted to underwriter, assigned a territory, and all was well! Let's say I thought all was well, until the ugliness of racism came knocking at my door. After the promotion, I began to interact with other business associates beyond my training cohort and office colleagues.

My territory comprised eight midwestern states. After about two years, I was promoted again to senior underwriter. As part of this new role, I set a traveling schedule to visit my customers to discuss their respective plans of coverage for the next policy year. I was excited about my upcoming client visits. I had worked closely with one particular agent writing new business and retaining existing business. I flew into the main airport and had to take a prop plane to my final destination for an overnight stay. The memory of that trip is forever etched in my mind, and, until the writing of this book, it weighed heavily on my heart.

It began early one morning several years ago with the worst and only prop plane experience of my life. I was one of only seven individuals—all men, except me—on the flight. The plane started its ascent into a bright, beautiful blue sky. I halfway listened to surrounding conversations as I began to plan ahead for my own business once the plane landed.

All of a sudden, we encountered a huge storm. The turbulence felt like an uncontrollable rocking chair as we floated back and forth across the sky. We were separated from the pilots by a mere curtain—they were part of the early-morning conversation as we boarded the plane. The talking dissipated into an eerie silence. The pilots closed the curtain as they diligently fought to stabilize the plane. We were on a roller coaster ride that turned into a flight of horror.

I began to pray for the pilots—and everyone on the plane—for our safe arrival and for my family, asking God to allow me to live for them. I prayed for my daughter, who was only nine months old, and for my husband, her father, who cared for her while I traveled for work. I wanted to see her grow up, and I wanted to see them again. I promised God I would look for another opportunity that didn't require as much travel away from them if he allowed me to return home. I didn't think we would make it to our destination.

Isaiah 38:7

"This is the Lord's sign to you that the Lord will do what He has promised."

When we finally landed, the sun was shining brightly, and the rain subsided. I began to thank God for allowing us to arrive safely. The safe and secure arrival was God's affirmation of His promise. I felt a renewal within myself. God wasn't finished with me, and His plans for me would come to fruition. Above all else, He would allow me to be home with my family again. Still shaking uncontrollably from the morning's flight experience, I quickly walked to the only rental car kiosk to secure the car I reserved for my visit.

My first appointment was an hour drive from the airport, which gave me the opportunity to pray, calm down from the experience of that flight, and listen for God's direction after the activities of the morning. I also prayed for God to give me the peace I needed to handle the business before me with my clients. ***Isaiah 41:10***

"So do not fear, for I am with you; do not be dismayed for I am your God. I will strengthen you and help you; I will uphold you with my righteous right hand."

It is during times like this that we are to fear not and remember God is with us, working it all out for good. Allow God's word to strengthen you while He carries you through your journey. It's not easy, but it's necessary. Let God know you stand on His word as you move forward in your life's journey.

I arrived at my client's office in one piece—hungry, but in one piece. The unexpected delay in our flight forced me to travel to my first appointment during my lunch hour with no time to stop for a quick salad to eat along the way to their office. I quieted my spirit and felt positive about the upcoming meeting. I remember thinking, *I have arrived.* All the hard work paid off: married; a healthy and beautiful baby girl; a home; and a great job with excellent benefits and coworkers. God brought me a mighty long way! What else could I possibly expect, need, or want?

As I walked into the office, my primary contact in the agency was a customer service representative. She was happy to see me, and likewise, I was happy to see her. We had shared so many telephone conversations over the months leading up to my visit that it seemed as if we were becoming close business friends. We shared normal pleasantries and talked about our families before we began to discuss the accounts. Neither she nor the agent had eaten lunch before I arrived; unexpected circumstances occurred in their office while I was on the "flight of horror." We briefly talked about going for a late lunch if time permitted after our visit. We had arranged to tour four different client locations to continue building client relationships and increase the probability of remaining their future commercial insurance carrier.

While in college, I worked as a peak-time teller for one of the local financial institutions where I realized the importance of getting to know your customers and providing great customer service. As an underwriter, I already knew the importance of external relationships. However, I gained great knowledge about myself. I was intrigued by others and their life stories. I really enjoy learning about other people's stories.

Prior to leaving for our tour, I stopped by the agent's office to introduce myself and update him on all the appropriate accounts. Although each of the clients we planned to visit were from the same industry, they were unique in the way they handled risk management and risk avoidance. While visiting, I would receive an upfront view of their operations and speak with management about their areas of concern.

I was a multiple-lines commercial underwriter. Therefore, I handled all lines of coverage, including the worker's compensation insurance renewal of the accounts in my territory. Fortunately, and unfortunately, I had to deliver good and bad news if one of their accounts faced non-renewal due to the loss history of an account. As I entered his office, I noticed an elderly white man sitting across the room. He reminded me of a grandpa figure. Our initial discussion was very upbeat and nonthreatening. We appeared to be on the same page as we discussed the renewal premiums for his accounts. I looked down at my watch and thought to myself, *We will be able to grab lunch together after the client visits because our conversation is going along so well.* I admit my appetite quickly returned after the events of the morning flight.

The last topic to discuss was the worker's compensation portion of the accounts. Unbeknownst to me, I was about to receive a huge dose of reality. The accounts we discussed were ones with a heavy lifting requirement for their employees. This requirement increased the exposure to back injuries for a specific group of their employees. I expressed to him that while a couple of the accounts experienced marginal losses, we could work with our Loss Control Department to mitigate those.

Without any warning to his tone shift, he told me "the niggers" were the ones lifting the products, and they didn't care about them hurting their backs. I must have turned every shade of red in the crayon box. After a moment of disbelief, I immediately replied, "Excuse me. I think I misunderstood. Please repeat what you said."

He reiterated exactly what I thought I heard him say the first time. My mind met the comment with incredulity, and my heart sank into my stomach. I remember quickly thinking to myself, *In this day and time, who thinks this way anymore?* Unfortunately, racism was alive and well and still exists today.

While I experienced hardship as a biracial person all my life, I had never been in the presence of anyone who used the "N" word in a derogatory manner in front of me. I was speechless as time stood still. Did this man not know I was a black woman? Did he care that I was a black woman? The customer service representative who I had developed a close business relationship with entered the room just as he repeated himself. She interrupted his comments, providing him relief from additional sentiments by suggesting we would be late if we didn't leave. She suggested we continue the worker's compensation conversation during our late lunch. The agent seemed unaware of the offense I felt, and he insisted I return to his office after our tour so we could all eat together and finish discussing the issues of that particular account. The customer service representative and I left the office to meet our first client. After that first client visit, I walked to my rental car. I immediately called my husband to tell him about the meeting.

He asked, "What did you say?"

I told him I didn't confront him due to the interruption of the customer service representative and that I quickly became preoccupied with ensuring my safety. My thoughts went very quickly to my hour-plus drive back to the airport. I didn't feel comfortable. I felt that if I said anything, I might not make it back to the airport if I made his comments an issue. As I talked with my husband, the realities of life rolled around in my head. I knew the history of my people. There is a long history of black people killed because of the color of our skin. I knew about the unjust treatment received at the hands of those who simply didn't care about black people and felt we were inferior just because the color of our skin was different. I was well aware of the lynching and perception of black people in the south. We were only good enough to be the slaves of our oppressors.

I quickly snapped back to the situation at hand. I was afraid for my life. I didn't know anything about the city or the people living there. Normally, I am a fighter, standing up to these types of situations, but God put it in my spirit to be at peace, for this battle was His.

I returned, and we finished our tour. We hopped in our cars to head back to the main facility. I immediately called the airline to see if there was another flight leaving for North Carolina, my home, that evening. There was one with a connecting flight in another city, but ultimately, it would reach my desired destination. I booked the flight, and I informed my associates of the change in my plans. I turned down the late lunch date so I could reach the airport in time to catch the last flight of the evening, instead of staying the night as originally planned.

That experience really rocked my foundation. It made me realize there is no arrival. The more things change, the more they remain the same. Change only comes about when everyone understands the change must happen within themselves. None of us are perfect. Therefore, there is room for all of us to change our perception of others, change the way we treat others, and stop tearing people down and seeking to destroy others. ***Psalm 121:7-8***

> *"The Lord will keep you from all harm—he will watch over your life; the Lord will watch over your coming and going both now and forevermore."*

I certainly was not expecting any of what unfolded throughout that particular day. As I settled back on the return flight home, I remembered the fear I felt most of that day. I remembered the anger I felt during my time in the agent's office. I remembered the horror I felt because of his prejudice. If *he* couldn't tell I was a biracial woman, what ethnicity did *others* believe I was?

Throughout that day, I prayed for God to be with me, lead me, and guide me. Even when I experienced the unfortunate conversation regarding someone's belief about my race, I listened to God's voice throughout the day to arrive safely back to my family.

Joshua 1:9

> *"Have I not commanded you? Be strong and courageous. Do not be afraid; do not be discouraged, for the Lord your God will be with you wherever you go."*

ಲ Pause and Reflect ಲ

There are so many things which happen that are out of our control. Hurtful thoughts, words, and actions happen ultimately out of ignorance. Ignorance of how their actions hurt others and the impact the ignorance will have on others sometimes causes their actions to be adopted and duplicated toward others because they are unable to discern the implications of such behavior. I have experienced humiliating situations like this more times than I care to admit, but I suggest that you not focus on the humiliating actions of others. I would ask you to approach such situations with humility. Humility allows you to walk forward into God's power. It prevents you from getting stuck in a place designed to tear you apart. Have you experienced areas of racial tension or disparaging thoughts of others regarding someone's race or ethnicity? Take out your journal to answer the questions below. Capture the feelings you had about the scenario(s) and also include how you felt as an individual. How did you handle the situation? Were you accepting of such behavior? If you could do it over, would you change your actions or perception?

1. Have you ever prayed about something, and God provided it immediately? Or did it seem to take forever for you to get it? Are you still waiting for God to answer some of those prayers?

2. How did you handle the unexpected events that happened in your life? Did you take the power of God with you, or did you try to handle it alone?

3. Have you experienced something as traumatic as my experience with the insurance agent? How did you overcome it?

4. Have you wondered why God allows us to have these experiences? Why do you think things aren't perfect all the time?

5. What influence do you have to counter others' potentially traumatic experiences?

9

Promises

There were several promises I made to God during the "flight of horror." Did I keep them? I promised to be a beam of light for those who diligently sought to be their best selves. Was I upholding that promise?

During my time as a member of my company's team, individuals with aspirations of advancement in the company stopped by my office periodically to discuss their desires for recognition of their contributions. Most conversations usually referenced how they were slighted during a performance appraisal or promotion. The individuals wanted to know what they could have done differently to achieve the results they wanted. I shared my perspective on the importance of being the best individual you can be, which led me to one opportunity after another. Having the opportunity to meet and discuss with coworkers from various disciplines and professions within the office, all with diverse backgrounds, perspectives, and approaches was invaluable to me. The promise I made to make a difference in others' lives through sharing my perspective is important to me.

While I listened and shared with them, I learned so much from each person. The opportunity to discuss and see vulnerability up close and in person and empathize with the needs and desires of everyone who confided in me made me understand that people are more alike than we are different.

The bottom line is everyone wants to succeed. I saw firsthand the dreams and desires of individuals who wanted to achieve, who wanted the best, no matter the color of their skin. I had the opportunity to see hardworking individuals who wanted to be recognized for their work and accomplishments.

Be mindful of letting others define your success. Your manager might not give you a deserved promotion or raise. Strive to go above and beyond even when this happens to you. The way you decide to handle the situation will allow God to use situations like this for your good. Deciding this up-front allows you not to fall prey to allowing others to define who you are as a person and what you are capable of accomplishing. Unfortunately, there are people who will not be fair to you for various reasons. You may have a manager or supervisor with their own agenda. God knows these people exist; God has plans for you that no one can derail.

People and situations such as these are put in your path to develop you for the future opportunities God has for you. I shared my path and how I was able to move forth despite the obstacles I faced with anyone who would listen to me. I continued to be a beam of light, sharing God's goodness with anyone sharing my journey.

Looking back over my own life, and as my three daughters moved through elementary school, middle school, high school, college, and every other facet of their lives, I am amazed that the more time passes, the more they remain the same. Seeing them experience some of the very same issues and situations is heartbreaking. Why does it have to be this way? I say it doesn't. We all can make a difference. It simply starts with following God's commandments.

This world will try to make you feel like you have power when you believe you are better than those around you. We are led to believe we are better because of our skin color, the number of degrees we earn, the specific job title we hold, or even our birth family. Maybe you have more money than your neighbor, and you feel that defines you and allows you to negate others because they are not like you. Is this what better should look like? Don't allow society to define the works God requires of you as a successful person. Blaming others for their misfortune makes it easier not to accept what God says is required for those entrusted with much. ***Luke 12:48***

> *"But the one who does not know and does things deserving punishment will be beaten with few blows. From everyone who has been given much, much will be demanded; and from the one who has been entrusted with much, much more will be asked."*

Conversely, this world will also try to make you feel like you are not good enough for any number of reasons. Maybe you don't have what you desire the most—maybe it's material possessions, money, a lot of friends, a husband, a wife, children, a college education, or the career you want. Again, the list of why you aren't good enough could go on and on. We blame our issues or lack of success on everyone else around us, making it much easier not to become the person we are destined to become. ***Matthew 7:3***

> *"Why do you look at the speck of sawdust in your brother's eye and pay no attention to the plank in your own eye? How can you say to your brother, 'let me take the speck out of your eye,' when all the time there is a plank in your own eye?"*

Work distractions also try to keep us from receiving God's promises. Often, I reflect on the comments the agent made to me about not caring about the injuries of "the niggers" while we met in his office a couple of decades ago. The pain of that one word, and all it symbolizes for so many people, is forever etched in the mind, body, and soul. This word creates a chasm between people that denies the acceptance and gift of giving love. Over time, I learned most people desire to be loved and accepted.

God gave us the desire to be loved from the very beginning of time. He spoke to the Sadducees and Pharisees when they tested Him, asking, "Teacher, which is the greatest commandment in the Law?" We are to love the Lord our God with all our heart, mind, and soul. God's response can be found in **Matthew 22:37-39**.

"Love the Lord your God with all your heart and with all your soul and with all your strength and with all your mind and love your neighbor as yourself."

I promised God I would love people regardless of the color of their skin, to look at their character and their heart, to listen to the words they use to speak to and about others, and, yes, to treat people as I want to be treated.

This world is so complex with many issues and concerns. Always remember that you likely are unaware of what others are going through in their life based solely on their appearance. I choose to live my life as my mother taught me. If you can't say anything nice to someone, don't say anything at all. My husband and I taught our daughters the same. However, please be aware that you will encounter others who will not value this about you and will speak negative and false words about you. Please understand this negative reaction doesn't have anything to do with you. This God-given power allows you to handle situations like this in a manner that some may fear.

The other promise I made on the "flight of horror" was to pursue an opportunity where I didn't have to travel several states away so I could be a presence in my children's lives. I did not want to miss chunks of my daughters' lives while traveling for work. God provided another opportunity of growth for me with another company, and I kept my promise. The opportunity looked and felt different, but I knew God was leading me along the path He wanted me to follow.

Growth occurs during the act of keeping promises. We learn, and we adjust our ideas, thoughts, and mindset as we pursue God's greatest commands. People are hurting in this world, and some of them want you to hurt just as much. So, they harm or offend you to cover up their own personal pain. Usually, you can identify these people within a few minutes of meeting them. We are to love them anyway; you don't need constant contact with negative or destructive people, unless God calls you to influence their life. If He gives you such an assignment, you will know right away. Choosing forgiveness is for you and your wellbeing.

☙ Pause and Reflect ❧

First, think about scenarios in your life where you struggled to forgive someone's actions. Recall how you felt about the individual(s) before the offense, during the offense, and after you decided to move on from the specific situation without forgiving them. Next, think about situations where you have chosen to forgive someone's actions against you. How did forgiveness allow you to move on with a clear heart, mind, and conscience to the plans God has for you? Reflect on this and your responses to the following questions.

1. Have you made promises to God? Have you kept those promises?

2. What compelled you to follow through on those promises?

3. Do you carry the burden of emotional baggage that belongs to someone else? Is their baggage preventing you from moving forward with your plans?

4. Is personal baggage, whether yours or someone else's, keeping you from developing a closer relationship with God?

5. Is obedience an important part of your relationship with God? In this context, what does obedience mean to you?

10
ও ♥ ও

Fulfillment

While my experience with racial ignorance—from the agent with whom I wanted to build a professional relationship—was unpleasant, it was a defining moment in my life. I chose not to let it delay my so-called arrival as a wife, a mother, and a successful contributor to my community. I would not let it hinder me from achieving my goals and the opportunities life offered.

Choosing to move forward was the only choice for me. I was disappointed, but I refused to get stuck in a never-ending loop of wondering what happened in his life to harden his heart toward an entire race of people. God used this particular situation to prepare me for so many others I experienced along my journey. This is the reason I can stand firm on God's word and tell you to use the potential setbacks as opportunities to move forward in your own life.

We were never promised we would not have trials or tribulations. What is most important is how you handle the adversity of life.
James 1:2-5

> *"Consider it pure joy, my brothers and sisters, whenever you face trials of many kinds, because you know that the testing of your faith produces perseverance. Let perseverance finish its work so that you may be mature and complete, not lacking anything."*

You have likely encountered, just as I have, those individuals who discourage you from pursuing an opportunity because you aren't prepared, or good enough, or any of a number of reasons they would like you to believe about yourself.

Again, keep moving forward. Those naysayers didn't make you, so neither can they break you. God is your maker, and He put so many qualities inside of you to discover your own success. Individuals who don't want you to succeed or grow beyond them aren't people you want in your life. You want people in your life who are happy for you and your success. Be mindful of the people with whom you share your hopes and dreams because some may work against you and your aspirations.

When God places someone in your life to assist you along your journey, He allows you to recognize who He placed before you. They are happy for you, they will assist you with your success, and they will listen without giving you reasons why you shouldn't pursue your dreams. They will share their success and failures as lessons for you to consider along the way. They aren't threatened by your success.

You might say, "God hasn't sent anyone to share in my journey forward." Maybe He hasn't, and maybe He has, but this I know from **Romans 8:28:**

"And we know that in all things God works for the good of those who love Him, who have been called according to his purpose."

Keep moving forward with the assurance that God is with you always, even when you don't feel or see Him working in your life. You have the power to decide the outcome of your pursuits. Always remain in possession of that power, and never give it away to those who don't want you to succeed.

The awakening I received during the visit in the agent's office made me realize there is no "arrival" in life. We are a constant work

FULFILLMENT

in progress. Ditch the expectation of arrival and begin the process of becoming the best version of yourself. If you deferred pursuing your dreams, I encourage you to pick them back up and pursue them again.

☙ Pause and Reflect ☙

Do you personally feel fulfilled in your life? If not, what is lacking? I encourage you to answer the questions for this chapter in your journal and capture any thoughts you may have about the delayed actions you experienced. While you write, identify a couple of steps to help you get back on track to accomplish your dream deferred.

1. Do you believe you have reached the pinnacle of your life? Do you believe you are a constant work in progress?

2. Have you become the person God created you to be?

3. What would you change about yourself? What prevents you from embarking upon a journey to become your best?

4. Do you have dreams and aspirations to be more and love more? Do you want more for you and your family? Are you willing to do the work to make those dreams come to fruition? Do you allow the opinions of others to prevent you from pursuing your dreams?

5. Have you given up on your dreams? What will your life look like if you don't actively pursue your dreams? What will your life look like if you pursue those dreams today?

11
Knowledge and Fortitude

Accepting God's mandate to move forward regardless of what I am faced with allowed me to see beyond the ugliness of the ignorance of the comments made in the agent's office that day. It also allowed me to realize the power retained in forgiveness. My husband and I decided we wanted to have two additional children and planned our careers around them, while serving our community, desiring to be a light for God. We also decided to be present and involved in our daughters' lives. After all, God answered our prayers to become parents, so we owed it to Him to be the best for them. Leading our family by example is how we parent.

One day, our oldest daughter came home from school upset about a situation with one of her classmates. I found myself telling her exactly what I was taught as a child. "If you cannot say anything nice to someone or about someone, don't say anything at all." I also discussed with her how some people are not taught to be kind to others and that sometimes people act out toward others because they are hurting. Their pain allows them to act out, forcing that same pain upon others. Teaching our daughters to always be the better person when there is dissension around them came from the desire to raise our daughters the way God commands.

We taught our daughters to value people for their character and not by the color of their skin. Making the decision to raise them this way unknowingly subjected them to a lot of pain from others. As a parent, I felt every experience they felt. Looking back as my daughters grew up, I relived situations I experienced. There were so many parallels between my daughters' stories and my own.

We were beyond excited when our oldest daughter went to college. She persevered through her studies and was accepted to one of the top universities in the country. Move-in day was bittersweet for our family. For any of you who have dropped your child off at a college or university and have been told by experts that it's best to cut the ties and let them become self-advocates, you know how difficult this can be. You led by example, hoping they understood your unconditional love.

Even though she always wanted to attend and diligently approached her studies to be admitted to this particular university, we were naturally apprehensive about letting her go and following the experts' advice. We waited for her to call us. It was one of the saddest times in our household. I remember one night as we prepared for bed, my husband was having a very difficult time and really missing her. I reminded him we prepared her for this opportunity all of her life, and she would be fine. And we would be as well. He replied, "Yes, we prepared her, but we did not prepare ourselves."

It appeared we had done our duty as parents because we didn't hear from her until several weeks after she arrived on campus. All was going well, or so I thought. One evening after dinner, she called my cell phone. I was so excited when I saw her name come across the caller ID! However, when I answered, I could hear the despair in her voice.

She cut right through the small talk and said, "Mom, why would someone say, if slavery was still happening today, I would be a house slave?" We did not teach our children to choose their friends based upon their race. We taught them to choose their friends based upon their values, morals, and character. She explained that another student of African descent told her she wasn't black. In front of their newly developed friend group, he began to question who she was as an individual.

Her classmate began to talk with her about house and field slaves, implying that my daughter would have been a house slave because of her light-skinned complexion. Historically, owners of slaves categorized their slaves into groups, creating a schism among the people still alive today. The slaves who performed laborious agricultural work six or seven days a week from sunup to sundown during rain or shine were called the field slaves. The slaves who performed the domestic duties of the house for the master and his family were called the house slaves. It was thought the mixed-race, lighter skinned slaves who were conceived by sexual depredation of the master of the plantation were perceived to be more desirable and mostly worked as domestic slaves. There was also a belief that they brought a greater profit for the owners selling them.

Our daughter was taught and learned about the ugliness of slavery at a very young age. She even visited and walked the grounds of the plantation where my husband's ancestors were enslaved. We taught our daughter history beyond what was discussed in school about slavery. I never imagined she would encounter this type of assault on her race or ethnicity at this point of her life. It felt like a different time and place. After all, hadn't our society and its people moved so far beyond my experiences? I guess not.

Later that evening, we discussed all of her concerns. Ultimately, I told her she couldn't let someone define who she was as an individual. I began to name all the characteristics she possessed and reminded her of the beautiful person she was, both inside and out. I also told her she had no control over who God used to bring her into this world; just like me, she could not choose her parents or grandparents. ***Jeremiah 1:5***

"Before I made you in your mother's womb, I knew you. Before you were born, I chose you for a special work."

The color of your skin doesn't make you the person that you are. It's your values, morals, character, desire to help, and ability to accept responsibility for your actions and not blame others for who or where you are in life.

I remember hanging up the phone call from my daughter that fall evening with so much sorrow because she had so much hope for her college experience. She thought she would be judged by her intellect and her desire to make a difference in someone's life. She had to come to a place where she could accept who God made her and make the decision to move forward to His plan before her.

However, as a mother and someone who experienced the same degree of scrutiny because of the color of my skin, my heart ached for her and so many others who are judged unfairly because of their appearance.

We are called to love ourselves just as God and Jesus loves us. *1 John 4:8*

> *"Whoever does not love does not know God, because God is love. This is how God showed his love among us. He sent his one and only Son into the world that we might live through Him."*

Keep moving forward toward the goals and plans you have for yourself, taking one step at a time. You will be amazed as God opens doors for you to walk through and closes those which must be closed for you to move forward.

While our oldest daughter experienced others attempting to make her question her identity at college, our middle daughter also experienced some of the same types of issues at school. She and her best friend decided they were interested in being boyfriend and girlfriend. They were both mature beyond their middle school age. He told his parents he was interested in her as a girlfriend. His mother and I discussed the situation and felt it would be okay to let them develop a relationship beyond friendship. We assured each other that everything would be okay.

It went smoothly for a while, but then they began to be bullied about their relationship because he was white and she was black. Her peers did not like the idea of them dating and made their relationship an issue. My heart broke for the two of them. All the bullying caused my daughter to pull back from the friendship *and* relationship because she couldn't believe the reactions of those around her. It was something every day.

He was really mature beyond his years because he told her the other friends wouldn't matter as long as he had her friendship. The other students won in this situation; they were too young to understand and overcome the dynamics of such a strenuous situation. I gave her the exact same advice I gave my eldest daughter. I told her she couldn't let anyone define who she was as an individual. I began to name all the characteristics she possessed and reminded her of the beautiful person she was, both inside and out. I told her she had no control over who God used to bring her into this world; just like me, she could not choose her parents or grandparents. I also told her to love individuals who love her and not let the color of someone's skin deter her from pursuing a loving and meaningful relationship when she was ready to embark upon finding her future husband.

My youngest daughter is currently in her fourth and final year of her undergraduate studies in college. During her freshman year, she chose to become a member of the black student organization on campus with a desire to meet other black students with the same interests as her, despite being ostracized by a group of girls who were members of the student organization because of her lighter skin tone. She was so excited to be among so many different people in the group and was asked to be an ambassador for the organization. Facing the same ridicule as her older sisters due to her skin tone, she rebuked how others tried to make her feel bad about who she was as a person because of the color of her skin. I commend her for the strength she showed for participating in this group and not allowing others to put her in a proverbial box and prevent her from participating. Her experiences with acceptance far surpass the words written here.

However, just like her siblings, I reminded her often that one's existence is out of their control. God wanted her here, and He wanted her to be born just the way He wanted. He chose the parents He wanted to entrust her to for His glory. I asked her to remain open to the possibility of God showing her the greatest love through Him and to remain open to the path He laid out for her. *__John 15:9__*

> *"I have loved you as the Father has loved me. Now continue in my love. I have obeyed my Father's commands, and He continues to love me. In the same way, if you obey My commands, I will continue to love you. I have told you these things so that you can have the true happiness that I have. I want you to be completely happy. This is what I command you: Love each other as I have loved you."*

ꙮ Pause and Reflect ꙮ

Decide right now in this moment to move forward showing the light for God's glory. Let His commands move you on to love others as He requires on your way to your destiny. It would be so much easier to just roll with the punches delivered by life, accepting what others would want you to believe about who you are and what you can and can't do to ensure you don't realize the truths of God. Life will get tough, and some of the tasks you are trying to achieve will be met with great opposition. It is when you find yourself in this space that you will discover God has plans to make you prosper and not harm you. These plans will give you hope and a future.

1. Do the negative opinions of others about your abilities keep you from accomplishing your destiny? Do you have positive affirmations you can use when others try to impose their negative thoughts upon you? If yes, use them along with God's word to block the negativity of others.

2. Have you ever experienced being told you weren't good enough to pursue a career opportunity?

3. Has anyone expressed their disapproval of a relationship because of a difference in ethnicity or race?

4. Pray for God to show you that your weaknesses are perfected by His power. Will you trust God and move forward with Him?

12

Faith With Intention

Making the decision to move forward no matter the obstacles you face will allow you to see God's love for you up close and in person. Glimpsing back over my life, I am reminded of all the times I made the decision not to turn back but to move forward. I simply wouldn't give up. When I faced challenges, I first asked myself, "How can I accomplish this task?" I read, studied, and asked questions until I found an answer. Then I finished the task and moved forward.

I accomplished so many tasks, which were supposed to be out of my reach, with God's grace on my life. First, when medical odds were against me, and the doctors said, "You won't live," God had another plan. Not only did I live, I lived without any health issues and developed into a fully functioning member of society. Second, God gave me the ability to learn and become educated about the life around me. I am always seeking to better myself. God wants more for us and will help us achieve our goals if we stay the course and keep the faith in God's promises.

God allowed me to become a wife and a mother. I always put one foot in front of another with the same faith in God through my Savior Jesus Christ. There were of course roadblocks and detours along the way; it was not a straight line to success, but through it all, God kept me. Just when you think you have it all figured out, something will happen to change the dynamics of those elements you mastered and have under control. This is an attempt to make you distrust God's word and the plans He has for you.

While our oldest daughter was in college, we had two additional daughters that needed our guidance. While this is not a book about rearing children, I admit being a mother is one of the most challenging experiences of my life. As a mother, you want to protect your children from the people and obstacles that will bring them harm.

Throughout my journey, I realized my reputation as an individual is very important to me. If I commit to a task, I will get it done no matter what occurs. I suggest you adopt this acronym, DWYSYWD (Do What You Say You Will Do), and the mentality to see it through no matter what comes your way!

Recently, I worked full-time as the executive director for an organization, served as president of a different service organization to give back to my community, mentored students and employees, and served as a deacon in my church, in addition to the responsibilities as a wife and mother, and someone asked me, "How do you do it all?" My response was, "It's God's grace and mercy." I was able to successfully maneuver all of these roles because, in everything I do, I put God first. When I look back, I know, without a shadow of a doubt, God was working it all out for me. He gave me the assignments, so He gave me everything I needed to see those things through to fruition for His glory. Looking back now, I think to myself, *It is simply favor, God's favor, on my life!* I could not have fulfilled all of the requirements for those positions without God.

I desired to be so much more than the people around me expected or wanted me to accomplish. To this day, I still have the same desire: to be the best person I can be in all situations. God has put so much inside of me to be used for His glory. Accepting mediocrity is not an option for me. I learned the desire to be successful for God's glory doesn't change; the assignments become greater. After all, if He can trust you with little tasks, He will trust you with much. **Psalm 37:4**

"Take delight in the Lord, and He will give you the desires of your heart."

My suggestion is to accept God's love, grace, and mercy to help you along your journey. Before I truly understood the power of God's love for me, I always tried to handle life's challenges on my own. I had to learn God doesn't need my help to accomplish the desires of my heart. I prayed about it and then immediately developed a strategy to fix whatever was needed. It became so much easier when I decided to do just as His word says in **Matthew 11:29**

"Take my yoke upon you and learn from me, for I am gentle and humble in heart, and you will find rest for your souls. For my yoke is easy and my burden is light."

Jesus paved the way for you. God wants us to stand on His word. It does not matter what the circumstance looks like. He can turn it all around. That which was meant for evil against you will be made for good by God.

☙ Pause and Reflect ☙

Are you willing to accept His assistance to pave the way for someone else's life? I remember thinking God wanted me to live my life as a positive role model for my daughters, giving them an example to follow as they grew up and matured as young ladies. I had the opportunity to serve as a positive role model to so many other women that God brought into my life. God has put us here to make an impact on other individuals' lives. Simply put, it is not always about us. Pray for God to help you move past the hurt or pain caused by other situations or other people. Ask God for clarity to help you move to the point of assisting others.

1. Do you have unaccomplished goals or the desire to make an impact in other people's lives? What are they?

2. What did it take to succeed at other accomplished goals? Did you seek God's guidance along the way? Did you seek out the expertise of others to help you along your way to success?

3. Have you experienced failures in your life? Why do you consider them failures? Did you seek God's guidance while you were in the valley? Did you seek guidance during this time, or did you walk it out on your own?

4. Are you willing to share your experiences to assist someone along their journey?

5. Are you receptive to the plans God has for you?

13

Forgiveness

Have you ever experienced hurt feelings or intentional harm at the hands of someone else? Have you ever had to actively forgive someone for hurting you or causing pain in your life? Forgiveness is making the decision to release the hurt or harm you experienced from the actions imposed upon you. At the end of the previous chapter, I asked you to think about being in a place to help someone move forward in their lives—paving the way for someone even if you wronged them or they wronged you.

I am sure if you were to write about offenses experienced in your lifetime, you would fill the journal and probably need to start a new one. What if I asked you to write down the offenses you committed against others? Would those offenses fill up an entire journal, needing room for another one? Maybe or maybe not. We must consider both actions to determine how we hurt others and how others hurt us to stop allowing such behavior against you and to not inflict such behavior onto others.

Truthfully, I have found myself in the midst of both of these situations more than I care to admit. Of all the situations I experienced, there is one occasion that stands out from the others where a business partner and I were not in agreement about an important decision. It was such an unpleasant event in our partnership.

We made several attempts to come to an agreement. God showed His face to me during this particular time like I never experienced before. We were in the office of a client, one who had become a friend to both of us. Our client didn't want the team to split; we were doing great work together. During a meeting, we were asked how things were going. We still had issues to work out, and we weren't there yet. Our client offered to pray for both of us in his office. As he began to pray for us, God was definitely in the midst of the prayer session. After leaving the meeting, we decided to move forward with our partnership.

Over the next couple of weeks, even after praying with our client, I was not at peace. Everything seemed so chaotic surrounding our partnership. I did not have any joy or peace about the situation. As I walked our family dog one evening, I felt God tell me, "I am not a God of chaos and confusion." *1 Corinthians 14:33*

"For God is not a God of confusion but of peace."

We ended our partnership. As you can imagine, there were a lot of logistics to address and many hurt feelings because the partnership did not go as we anticipated.

I was disappointed, and the disappointment turned into anger. The anger began to take over who I was as an individual. I was not myself. Another evening while walking our dog, I decided to forgive my business partner for all the misunderstandings. I prayed as I walked and asked God to lift the burden from me. I forgave my business partner, and it was as if someone lifted 50 pounds from my shoulders. Yes, I carried what felt like half my body weight in resentment and hard feelings around on my shoulders. What a heavy burden from circumstances out of my control.

Controlling the actions of others is totally out of your control. However, you can control your own actions. I knew it was time for me to forgive and move forward. The lesson I learned was the power of forgiveness. I learned that forgiveness did not have much to do with my ex-business partner, but everything to do with me. The moment I decided to forgive and not hold it in any longer, the burden of that entire situation no longer controlled my thoughts, my being, or my destination. All the chaos ceased. I could move onto my next opportunity of growth.

While living in unforgiveness, I was unable to see God and the plans He set for me. Once I reached this point of forgiveness, I began to reflect on why this particular situation was so difficult for me. Certainly, I had been through situations of disappointment before. Why was this situation different? I realized when I encountered disappointment, heartache, and pain from someone's actions toward me in the past, I didn't hold onto the hurt. I forgave the people and the situations, and sometimes I forgave myself for falling into such circumstances.

Forgiveness allowed me to move forward past the pain. Why had I forgotten about the power of forgiveness? I dare to say I did not really know at that time the power forgiveness carried. God had to teach me just how powerful forgiveness is and how powerful it can be when you allow yourself to forgive. **Ephesians 4:31**

"Get rid of all bitterness, rage, and anger, brawling and slander, along with every form of malice. Be kind and compassionate to one another, forgiving each other, just as in Christ God forgave you."

Reflecting on why this mishap with my ex-business partner affected me so deeply, I realized I was holding onto all of the time and effort I put into making the business a success, along with the disappointment of learning that people won't always value the things you value and vice versa. We are all different because of our experiences.

When you can love an individual who has hurt you, this propels you forward along your journey. This love prevents you from holding someone else's baggage when it was never yours to hold.

As you grow into a place which allows you to forgive others, you will learn that forgiveness has more to do with you as an individual than you could imagine. It allows your heart to heal and progress to the greater tasks God has planned for you and your life. The weight you carry on your shoulders is lifted when you forgive. The unending film, which plays over and over in your mind, finally ends when you forgive. You can move forward with a clear mind and heart with the peace that passes all understanding.

If you never experienced the peace of forgiveness, let me tell you, you only rob yourself. If you are fortunate enough to never have been in such a situation, you have time to decide how you will handle it when you're faced with this challenge. If you are faced with a choice, choose to forgive those who trespass against you. This way you are prepared to forgive whatever comes against you.

Allow yourself the opportunity to open the door of forgiveness so you can move beyond these types of situations. Just as I did, allow the weight to be removed from your shoulders.

I have heard many people say, "I will forgive, but I won't forget." Really? Are you joking? My life experiences taught me that true forgiveness is found when you can forget all of it. Why wouldn't you forget? Holding onto even one morsel keeps you captured in the situation and sometimes tied to the very individuals who caused the hurt, pain, or unrest. Allowing yourself to forget allows you the freedom to move forward. Being unwilling to totally forgive past transgressions—either of yourself or someone else—will keep you stuck and unable to move forward.

I navigated the healing process of that failed business situation for about four months. That four months was four months too long. God was showing me little clues along the way, but I overlooked the signs right in front of me. The decision to move forward is yours.

ෆ Pause and Reflect ෆ

As you go through further self-reflection, you may rediscover situations that caused you a lot of hurt and pain in the past. Whatever you discover, please understand it's time to deal with and forgive them and move on to uncover the next opportunity of growth. Will you forgive and forget, or will you choose to stay in stagnation and deteriorate? In most cases, the other people involved have moved on while you are stuck in unforgiveness. Forgiveness affords you the ability to pray for someone who does seemingly irreversible damage to you or someone you love. Allowing yourself to achieve the act of forgiveness puts you front and center of where God wants you on this journey called life. Reaching this point of forgiveness allows God to freely work in our lives.

1. Are you dealing with any unresolved unforgiveness in your life? Have you offended someone, or has someone offended you?

2. Do you silently carry those unresolved issues along with you everywhere you go? How do they impact your ability to move forward?

3. Write out a plan of forgiveness for each of the items you listed. The plan can be as simple as deciding to let it go and forgive an individual or individuals or a situation or situations. You get to decide what the plan needs to look like for you!

4. Are you able to pray for or speak to people who have offended you? If so, this person or situation is no longer an area of concern for you.

14

Opportunity

After dissolving the partnership, I did not know what my next opportunity would be. I knew there would be a next opportunity to learn, grow, develop, and shine because when I forgave the entire situation and the weight was lifted from my shoulders, it was lifted from my mind. I was allowed to think about possibilities, and I could see opportunities as they presented themselves. I didn't realize someone had been watching me handle business situations during the partnership I had just ended. A woman asked me to join another team of individuals bringing my skills to assist some of the frailest people in our society: the elderly.

I met with the company's director of governmental relations and the chairman of the board to discuss joining their team. As I drove to our initial meeting, I remember talking with God, telling Him I really didn't want to attend this meeting. I kept giving Him excuses, as Moses did when God called him to serve.

As I drove into the parking lot of the restaurant, I commented to God, "First, I will know it's your will for me if in this meeting it seems like I have known these individuals all of my life. Second, this meeting will not be awkward, and third, when I leave, they will offer me an opportunity to be a part of their team."

Everything went well. I met two individuals I didn't know, and the other individual was an acquaintance. The conversation and interaction were absolutely amazing! It was as if we were lifelong friends. I didn't feel like a stranger, nor did they treat me like one. What was supposed to be a one-hour lunch turned into two, and as I left, they asked me for a proposal because they wanted me on their team.

What if I had decided not to forgive my previous business situation? Would I have missed the opportunity God was already working out for me? My belief is I would have missed this unforeseen opportunity because I would have been blinded by the circumstances of my failing partnership.

I trusted everything I knew about God and faith. Letting go allowed me to walk into the next opportunity. It allowed me to walk into a situation created by God. ***Matthew 21:21-22***

> *"And Jesus answered and said to them, 'Truly I say to you, if you have faith and do not doubt, you will not only do what was done to the fig tree, but even if you say to this mountain, 'Be taken up and cast into the sea,' it will happen. And all things you ask in prayer, believing, you will receive.'"*

God has shown up for me so many times in my life; again, on this day, He showed me His power. God provided for me during the meeting, and it was just as I asked of Him. He showed me my faith in Him was sufficient. While our faith may look different in every situation, He only requires faith the size of a mustard seed. ***Luke 17:6***

> *"And the Lord said, 'If you had faith like a mustard seed, you would say to this mulberry tree, 'Be uprooted and be planted in the sea'; and it would obey you."*

There are so many obstacles you can allow to keep you from accomplishing God's will for your life. However, it does not matter what may come your way. God's power through our Lord and Savior Jesus Christ will see you through. You have to believe there is a next opportunity for you, and you have to believe you deserve His gifts for you!

As I discussed in the previous chapter about the importance of forgiveness, when you forgive or are forgiven, you become ready and willing to accept all of God's plans for you. On my way to the meeting, I conceded to God and said, "Okay, God, if these things happen, then I know it is the will You have for me and my life for this time."

God was with me every step of the way as I joined an industry in which I never otherwise imagined I would become involved. I had the business acumen and skills necessary, along with the real-life experience of advocating for my mother when she became ill during the later years of her life. God is always preparing us. Even then, in the midst of my mother's illness, he allowed me to learn about the industry in a personal way. While assisting my mother, I learned about the medical and financial tools necessary to help maneuver through such a complex part of life.

The opportunity to learn about care of our most vulnerable population—the aged and aging—allowed me to develop a learned acumen of the policies and practices I would embark upon during the next part of my career. While researching care for my mother as she became sick, I began to learn about the industry. I never imagined God would call on me to learn, teach, advocate, and develop policy for this industry. It was not in my plans at all, but it is in times like this when I am reminded God is in control. ***Proverbs 19:21***

> *"Many are the plans in the mind of a man, but it is the purpose of the Lord that will stand."*

Just like me, you may not know your next opportunity, but God will disclose His purpose for you and your life. Purpose is not stagnant. We are always evolving in situations as God is developing us into the individuals He created us to be for His glory. We are presented with opportunities and situations and allowed to move on to the next season to develop our story and testimony for the individuals God places before us.

My experiences were not presented to me in the exact same way as this opportunity, and my relationship with God and my Savior Jesus Christ allows me to say I know yours haven't either. The one constant I am assured of is that He will show up for you. Not necessarily when or how we think He should. God has His timing, and it is perfect. ***2 Peter 8-9***

> *"But do not let this one fact escape your notice, beloved, that with the Lord one day is like a thousand years and a thousand years like one day. The Lord is not slow about His promise, as some count slowness, but is patient toward you, not wishing for any to perish but for all to come to repentance."*

When I was the executive director of a particular organization, I had a vacant position available within my office. We needed a marketing person to round out our team to ensure we were adequately staffed to provide the needed services for the members of the association. I already met with several potential candidates to fill the position and had two individuals left to interview before choosing someone to offer the position. Over the span of my career, I participated in numerous interviews seeking to find the best candidate for a position. The experiences of those interviews allowed me to develop my own thoughts about choosing a candidate who will flourish in a particular situation.

When interviewing, I am very interested in the growth mindset of a potential candidate. I often use the answer to the following question as a gauge of the candidate's growth ability. "If you had an opportunity to interview for my job as your manager, would you interview for my job?"

Typically, most people say, "No." I am usually concerned when individuals answer the question in the negative because when taking a position without considering the possibility for growth, you risk becoming complacent. For as long as I can remember, as a working teen up until the present, I always thought about growth and development because it is in each role that you are being prepared for your next opportunity.

The last candidate I interviewed that day for the position said, "Yes! I certainly would enjoy the opportunity to interview for your job." She explained how she planned to learn the job she was hired to do and carry out the responsibilities to the best of her abilities. Once she learned those duties, she would learn other areas to become a leader in the office, and if the opportunity presented itself, she would apply for my job. I ended up hiring her. She was looking for a challenge and the opportunity to grow, and she expected to grow in and beyond the current role. I know, just as she knew, when you are ready for the next move, it presents itself, even if you aren't looking for it.

☙ Pause and Reflect ☙

Do you have faith enough to know, even though you don't see or feel God working in your life, that He is working it all out for your good? Are you open for God to move you on to your next job, business, or faith experience? What's holding you back from pursuing your next opportunity for growth? Your next opportunity is waiting for you to arrive on the scene. Are you willing to walk forward into it?

1. Can you see God working in your life?

2. Are you willing to relinquish control to God?

3. Are you ready to move to the next level of your journey? If yes, and you haven't invited God into your life and accepted Jesus as your Savior, this is the time. His word doesn't say it will be easy, but it says He will be with you always.

4. What are your areas of concern? How do they prevent you from having a relationship with God? How do they prevent you from moving forward?

5. Are your prayers and plans for yourself in alignment with His will for your life?

15

Preparation

Waiting for God's timing to remove you from an undesirable situation is not easy. Perhaps your coworkers don't understand you. Maybe you discovered that someone with your exact job title makes more money than you, and yet you outperform them. Or you are the last still to be promoted after everyone around you has already advanced. Endless possibilities exist for you to insert here.

When you find yourself in this place, it's time for an honest conversation with yourself. Are you growing and expecting growth in your situation? In my career, when I looked for my next opportunity, I began to pray and understand why I wasn't experiencing growth in certain areas of my life. God was trying to bring me closer to Him. I couldn't quite understand why I was in that space. After all, God brought me a mighty long way. He kept me through all the challenges that could have destroyed me. There were many instances where others tried to hurt, harm, or cause danger to me, but God covered me.

I was taking care of business. I prayed, and I pursued God through my daily Bible study before leaving for work. I spread myself so thin. I said yes to everyone out of my desire to help them. I was running on empty. Why would I find myself in this place? I shouldn't have been where I found myself at that moment. However, I found myself there because, after some self-reflection, I understood I was relying on myself, and I wasn't seeking God's guidance as I moved forward. My relationship with God was suffering. I also learned God would meet me if I just kept moving forward. There was a time when I found myself at a crossroads during my career. It seemed as if I had applied for 100 positions and participated in over 50 interviews, just to be told I was overqualified or underqualified.

I kept praying and seeking God's face. I continued to move forward in every area of my life, even helping others while it didn't seem opportunities would align for me. I gave complete control of the situation to God, and the doors began to open. During this time, I learned some of the most valuable lessons in my life regarding obedience.

First, life happens in God's timing. Second, I learned the entire experience wasn't about me. It was and is about God's plan for my life. I had to keep the faith and pour into other people and situations. I knew, no matter how it seemed, He would work things out in His timing. It was not easy on my way to this realization. The doors for everyone around me were open with opportunities for them to pursue. I knew God was making plans all around me, which meant He was very close to me, but there was more for me to do before He would further open the doors intended for me. I had allowed the behavior of other people to harden my heart. I was guarded. I had forgotten His promise. He wanted me to let my defenses down and rely on Him just as I had previously in countless other situations.

Many scriptures we learn along our Christian journey are relevant as we face difficult times in our life. I began to lean on **Matthew 11:29-30**.

> *"Take my yoke upon you and learn from me, for I am gentle and humble in heart, and you will find rest for your souls. For my yoke is easy, and my burden is light."*

God loves us, and He wants His children to have the desires of their hearts.

PREPARATION

While I went into this particular season of my life, it tested my faith like nothing had before. I realized I was being tested and prepared for the next opportunity at the same time. God wanted me to give up control and to trust Him! There is so much value in learning the circumstances in your life may not be about you but instead about others and how you can help them as you walk your journey toward unselfishness. It also will help you see that what others do isn't always about you but about the person inflicting ill will because of their own lack of confidence in themselves.

Make the decision right now to move forward when this happens, so you can accomplish the plans God has for you. The next opportunity, promotion, or business opportunity usually shows up when you are helping others obtain their next growth experience, not while you seek what God can do for you. God calls us to help others. Putting others before yourself isn't always easy; work on one kind act at a time.

While you serve others, you should not expect anything in return. The ability to humble ourselves while helping others allows God to create in us the person He called us to be, Christ-like in every area of our lives. We are called to sacrifice for others, forgive others, forgive ourselves, create peaceful relationships where there is strife, and have more love in our heart for others. It doesn't matter how our relationships got offtrack; you are called to make it right and work for others to see God's light shine in you.

You may say, "I don't have a lot of anything to give anybody right now. I'm burnt out; I need everything I have, and I don't own anything I can share with anyone. I'm barely making it myself." If these thoughts come to your mind, step outside of thinking about yourself and develop a way to help someone. Sometimes, prayer is all you may have to give someone. Praying for someone is one of the most selfless acts you can do for others. Praying for your loved ones and your enemies alike shows a spiritual maturity, which pleases God. God knows when you pray for others. He knows when you put others' needs before your own, and this pleases Him. God's second greatest command is for us to love others as we love ourselves.

If you discover the majority of your time is spent on meeting your own desires, I challenge you to prioritize someone else outside of your family and watch how God will show up on your behalf. ***1 Corinthians 13:4-7***

> *"Love is patient and kind. Love is not jealous, it does not brag, and it is not proud. Love is not rude, it is not selfish, and it cannot be made angry easily. Love does not remember wrongs done against it. Love is never happy when others do wrong, but is always happy with the truth. Love never gives up on people. It never stops trusting, never loses hope, and never quits."*

I know this to be true because I lived it during this particular season of my life. My schedule was full of accommodating requests others made of me. God met me and allowed me to complete these requests as well as my own personal commitments. He allowed me to serve others with the skills and talents He placed inside of me. I know without a doubt that I was able to see those tasks through because of His grace.

One morning, as I opened the door to my office, I had this overwhelming feeling God was working on my behalf. I remember sitting at my desk, saying, "God, I know you are working something out for me, and whatever it is, I will go for you." Within several weeks, the next opportunity of service presented itself. I was called upon to sit on a board with the mission to minimize barriers to high-quality, accessible post-secondary education opportunities. As a governing board, we were responsible for improving the lives and well-being of individuals through ensuring their ability to obtain additional education, training, and retraining for workforce needs. In addition, we supported economic development through services and partnerships with businesses and industries to serve the communities and improve the overall quality of life.

It's amazing how God works! By this time, it seemed like an entire lifetime ago. Several years prior, my husband and I owned a preschool; a lot of our focus was preparedness for kindergarten and elementary school. The mission was for the graduates of our preschool to be ready to excel in elementary school. Many of those students were reading, writing, and already accomplished at the kindergarten level as they left our preschool to enter kindergarten. Our focus centered around the fact that the first five years of a child's life are often called the most formative years; these years are critical for development, performance, and overall success throughout their life.

Our preschool embodied this precept and provided the platform for the children's core learning and the success of the school. Those were the good old days, and we didn't even know it because it took a lot of hard work and perseverance to make the students and school successful. When asked to join this governing body, I realized the preparation was done when we were developing the programs and learning environment for our former students to be successful at the preschool level. God with His infinite wisdom provided me with the necessary skills to be a part of this governing body several years before this opportunity was presented to me. I knew the importance of education and its accessibility to those desiring to improve their life.

God prepares us all along the journey for those tasks He has for us to accomplish. I learned so much from this one opportunity, which I then successfully applied to the responsibilities and tasks in a new role for another opportunity. While you may not understand why you endure particular situations, it is to prepare you for what's next.

☙ Pause and Reflect ☙

Are you doing what you need to grow in every area of your life to prepare for God's next opportunity? Are you placing Him first, before all things? Do you have a desire to help someone with something that has nothing to do with you? If you can assist someone, even when you are experiencing challenges of your own, and providing assistance will not hurt or help you, it could be a test of obedience, trust, and faith.

1. What areas in your life do you continue to see growth? What are areas of stagnation?

2. Do you expect growth in those areas that aren't currently experiencing growth? If no, why not? Is your lack of attention or lack of expectation keeping you from growth?

3. Are you only focused on yourself and your needs? If yes, try doing something to improve someone else's situation. Take the focus off you and see what happens. Come back and journal about it later. Write about how it impacted your situation(s).

4. Can God trust you with a little so He can trust you later with a lot?

16

Personal Success

At some point in my life, I undeniably bought into the importance of multitasking, time management, and getting things done. Maybe you bought into some of the very same ideals as well. While possessing these qualities allowed me to accomplish a great deal of tasks on time, these very skills also made me miss out on real-life experiences. Several years ago, I had the distinct honor of speaking to a group of women. The message touched briefly on keeping the commitments we make, not only to others but to ourselves. The atmosphere in the room was infectious. It was full of buzzing conversations, and the people were excited to be in attendance. Some very important people gathered in the room, and pleasantries filled the air.

As I reviewed the agenda for the event, I discovered I was the next speaker. As I always do when speaking before a group, and sometimes when speaking to just one person, I invited God's presence to the conversation. I began to pray and ask God to speak through me. God knew who was there, and He knew specifically who needed a message from Him. I was God's willing vessel for His message to touch someone in the room.

As I stood at the podium, I gave some prepared remarks, along with some unprepared ones. I delivered the message and received a round of applause. Honestly, I remember checking the proverbial box next to this task as completed in my mind. This opportunity came during a very busy time in my life—a time when I was literally living my life via a calendar, sometimes without much emotion, checking tasks off as they were completed. I celebrated inwardly the feeling of task completion. I was elated to accomplish another call to serve through presentation.

If someone offered me a million dollars right this moment to recall the details of the presentation or the subject matter of my speech, I would have to turn it down. I don't remember the content of the message. I was so caught up in getting it done and checking it off my overcommitted list that I wasn't living the actual experiences God put before me for growth. I was in attendance, but I wasn't present.

Approximately four weeks later, it was a day like many others, jam-packed with to-do tasks before the next day's obligations began to take up time and thought. I accomplished my work morning priorities and realized my lunch hour was quickly approaching. During that hour, I had planned to leave my office, in the heat of a North Carolina midday, to register for a conference over the next three days.

After driving around several city blocks to find an available parking spot, a sense of relief came upon me as I approached the building and saw the registration line wasn't long at all. I could register in less time than it took to find a parking spot, and I could grab lunch before returning to work. This good fortune, coupled with visions of checking another task for the day, brought a sense of peace all over me.

This sense of relief, however, was interrupted as two pleasant and lovely ladies stopped me from entering the building. We exchanged greetings, and they told me they had attended my previous event four weeks ago—you know, the one I wouldn't receive a million dollars for because I couldn't recall the contents of the message? Yes, the one I checked off as complete.

The women complimented me on the presentation and the delivery of my message. They asked me how I delivered such an inspiring message with such calm and peace. Without any hesitation at all, I told them it was God speaking through me. He had given me the words to say. He knew the message needed by the people in the room. They went on to share that a light had shone all around me as I spoke that day. This was news to me! The ladies encouraged me to continue my work and rely on God as my guide because the remarks were excellent.

After meeting those two lovely ladies walking in to register for the conference, I really did not give much thought to the light they said emitted from me as I spoke at the previous event. I merely went about my life doing what I thought I was supposed to do for the glory of God; I was in a checkbox state of mind, meaning I was only going through the motions of life. Through all of the checking-off of calendars or lists and running from one obligation to another, God allowed me the opportunity to realize that all these tasks and functions were not about me. It was about Him and His glory, not just for me but for all those who love Him through Christ Jesus. We are allowed to accomplish tasks greater than our capacity when we have faith and trust in the Lord to see us through.

It was at that very moment that my feelings of being overlooked for personal and professional opportunities became less important than ever before. The real lesson was in what God was doing as I continued to move forward while serving others. Through it all, God was preparing me to serve Him in bigger ways. As my husband says, "I was getting seasoning."

It was amazing how God continued to work in my life. God was opening another door for me professionally. I remembered the prayer of Jabez in my own pursuit for God to enlarge my territory. ***1 Chronicles 4:10***

> *"Jabez cried out to the God of Israel, 'Oh, that you would bless me and enlarge my territory! Let your hand be with me and keep me from harm so that I will be free from pain.' And God granted his request."*

Another opportunity was offered to me because of the skillsets developed earlier in my career after graduating from college. Again, I was in awe of God's preparation and positioning of me for this opportunity. During this time, I began to think about all the people who were a part of my continued career growth. I contacted the vice president at the company who allowed me to pursue the trainee position. I thanked him for giving me the opportunity to grow professionally. He saw the potential I possessed and allowed me to pursue my dream job.

I am grateful to the individuals who saw my dedication, courage, and strength and who trusted me to honor God with the decisions I would face in the new position.

Some individuals were happy for my progression, and others were not. I remember attending church soon after receiving some negative reactions to me accepting this new career opportunity, one requiring the culmination of the skillsets developed along my professional journey. Our pastor delivered a message that Sunday morning, and I felt that he spoke directly to me. This all-powerful feeling began to take over my thoughts as I sat next to my husband in church. The pastor talked about not being jealous or envious of others' accomplishments, which they diligently pursued in their life. My mind and heart suddenly moved in full synchronization with an overwhelming feeling of relief.

As the pastor continued his message that morning, he shared with us the precept of not knowing what an individual goes through to get where they are in life. We don't know what they endure—the sleepless nights of studying for an exam, working two or three jobs to pay their way through school, or not having enough money to pay bills for the entire month. The list goes on with obstacles someone may overcome while working to reach their personal and professional goals.

During the sermon, I thought back to all that I had overcome to reach my place in life. I also thought about how very few people knew the full story of my plight to becoming successful. The desire to achieve more and be the best person I could has not been easy. Looking back over my life, I realized everything worth having or accomplishing is not easy. However, it is in the midst of these difficult challenges that we are made strong. It is during these situations you realize the growth you endure to reach the next milestone along your journey.

Psalm 27:1

"The Lord is my light and my salvation. Whom shall I fear? The Lord is the stronghold of my life. Of whom shall I be afraid?"

This scripture, along with the others included throughout this book, continues to be the strong foundation for my faith. God provided several opportunities I had been praying for all at once. I had recently accepted the call of deacon alongside my husband in our church. My spiritual maturity helped me understand those who were not happy with my success, and I prayed for them while they talked behind my back and created false narratives.

I discussed my feelings with someone and explained that I really did not expect anything different from those individuals. Why would I? Imperfect men crucified Jesus Christ. Why should we expect any different treatment from a mere man or woman today? You see, people will talk negatively and treat you differently as you grow and press toward the mark of becoming who God created you to be for His glory. Your growth scares people; maybe your growth allows them to see the stagnation of their own life. Maybe your growth prevents them from further manipulating you into a state of weakness. They are afraid once you become the best version of yourself, they will no longer have a hold on you and your ability to move on with your life. Finally, maybe they are afraid that same anointing that God placed upon you exists in them and that God is calling them forth to be the person He created them to be for His glory.

Satan and those people who allow themselves to be used by him will try to destroy you and anyone God has built up with gossip and lies. God urges you not to participate in the destruction someone tries to place upon you. ***Joshua 1:9***

> *"Have I not commanded you? Be strong and courageous. Do not be afraid; do not be discouraged, for the Lord your God will be with you wherever you go."*

During the service of my ordination as a deacon in our church, our pastor discussed how some believe, once you are a follower of Christ, you should expect life to be easier and problem-free. To the contrary, this is when it can become the most difficult because you made a decision to follow Jesus. When you commit yourself to following Christ, you can expect the most attacks against you in every area of your life with the goal of deterring you from your commitment to Christ. While Satan is after you, he is ultimately trying to attack God and His promise. I am a living testament of this message.

As a believer of Jesus Christ, you will encounter people designed to make your straight path crooked. ***Isaiah 45:2***

> *"I will go before you and make the crooked places straight; I will break in pieces the gates of bronze and cut the bars of iron. I will give you the treasures of darkness and hidden riches of secret places, that you may know that I, the Lord, who call you by your name, am the God of Israel."*

Through it all, God will see you through to salvation and victory. I know it's easier said than done because we have all found ourselves in these places at some time or another. When it seems like everything around you is not going the way you envisioned, when everything appears to go wrong, and when you face obstacles you never expected to, keep the faith. Don't give into the negativity imposed upon you by others or situations you did not anticipate. Use everything within you to keep moving forward and invite Jesus to go with you as you persevere to become the best version of who He created you to be for His glory!

1 Timothy 4:10

"That is why we labor and strive, because we have put our hope in the living God, who is the Savior of all people, and especially of those who believe."

Make the decision you will succeed and strive for the success that Satan is trying to keep you from accomplishing through Jesus. You can do it; with Christ, all is possible.

↭ Pause and Reflect ↭

Often times, I have wondered why some people are complacent with where they are, limiting expectations of themselves and often limiting expectations of the people or situations in their lives. We are not to be anxious for anything but through prayer and supplication make our requests known to God. In my spirit, I have always felt that I hadn't accomplished all God had for me. It is this longing that keeps me moving forward. I know His anointing is taking me to that destination. What message is your spirit delivering to you? Even in the midst of uncertainties and chaos, does your spirit tell you there is more? As you search your heart looking for that area where you can't be complacent, take out your journal and use it as a guide to assist you with uncovering obstacles to reach your personal success.

1. Have you ever been jealous or envious of another's success? If so, why?

2. How did this jealousy affect you and your ability to move forward? How did it make you feel?

3. Did you experience any positive growth from feeling jealousy or envy? Did others' success motivate you to work on yourself? If yes, in what ways? If not, why not?

4. Did the lack of growth make you rethink your situation? Did you consider alternative plans or paths to pursue your goals?

17
ഗ ♥ ഗ

The Light

One year, our family returned to our normal post-summer routine and prepared our daughters to go back to school. One was a sophomore in college and the other a senior in high school. Our firstborn was living life—she moved out after graduating from college and was working toward self-realization of her future goals. It was time to resume our regular routine.

It was just another Sunday morning at church, or so I thought. A lot of people stood and greeted one another, after not seeing each other over the summer vacation. As I walked back toward my seat, an associate minister approached me and said, "God told me to tell you not to be afraid. You know you are empowered for greatness. It is your season to rise and not to worry about your haters."

My quest to understand "the light" others had seen around me resurfaced because of this new message. I can remember the tears I fought back and the knot in my throat. Her message was met with my teary response: "I'm not afraid." It seemed as if the movie picked up right where it left off, with God speaking to me through someone else. I continued to be amazed by God's love, grace, and mercy in my life. I found myself at a loss because I had spent time over the summer thinking about God's next possible assignment. She told me not to be afraid. I told her I wasn't afraid. I really wasn't. I was more concerned with missing what God wanted. I began to research what it meant to be in the light from a spiritual perspective. I went straight to God's word for guidance. **Genesis 1:3**

"God said, 'Let there be light, and there was light.' And God saw that the light was good."

In God's word, light represents life and goodness. Light also symbolizes the holy God and God's presence and favor. This light dissipates darkness. Jesus came as the light of the world through His suffering on the cross for our sins. **John 1:4-5**

"In Him was life, and the life was the light of men. The light shines in the darkness, and the darkness has not overcome it."

I next talked with my pastor, who planned to retire and leave our church within the next couple of weeks. During our meeting, I shared with him all the messages I received from others regarding a light and doing great things for God. We discussed the process of God calling someone into ministry and my concern of missing His calling on my life. He told me to purchase a book he wanted me to read where I could find additional considerations about God's anointing on my life. Ultimately, though, if God was calling me to minister for Him outside of my duty as a deacon in the church, He would be relentless in His pursuit. I should stop worrying about missing my calling.

It was during our discussion I realized, as Christians, we are to be a light to the world. In everything we do, we are to let God's light shine through us for His glory. Your journey in serving God doesn't have to be as a pastor of the church. There are so many tasks, people, and situations we can be called to minister for God. **Matthew 5:14-16**

"You are the light of the world. A city set on a hill cannot be hidden. Nor do people light a lamp and put it under a basket,

but on a stand, and it gives light to all in the house. In the same way, let your light shine before others, so that they may see your good works and give glory to your Father who is in heaven."

There is always someone watching you as you live your own unique life. What will they see? Your disposition as you move forward will either encourage or discourage others as they move forward. Every day will look different than the day before. Both positive and negative circumstances will occur as you move forward. Embrace both on your way to victory for they each build resilience, character, and courage to see it through.

Life becomes much less complicated when we decide to be the best we can for God's glory. My best can be different than your best or the next person's best. So don't walk around comparing yourself to someone else's best, for God called each of us to specific tasks with the specific talents He gave us. Those talents continue to grow as we grow into the person God created us to be.

This lesson had been a long time coming for me. I agonized over missing God's calling. Seeking and finding the meaning of light collided with the fear of not being enough. God's light is victorious; I am enough, and you are enough. We are the light of the world until Jesus returns.

This book is a product of the light I embraced and chose to walk in with God's grace. Earlier in the book, I talked about not having the ability to complete this assignment given to me by God. During this season of seeking clarity about the light others saw around me, I learned through study of God's word that it is God's light that shines through us for all to see. It is His light that shines for people to see that His love, grace, and mercy is real and available to all who believe in His one and only begotten son, Jesus Christ.

As I write this chapter, we are deep into the COVID-19 pandemic, coupled with a time of unrest because of racial inequality and a cry for justice—a time of great health uncertainty and civil restlessness. It would be easy to simply act as if none of this is happening in this day and time. After all, we are too sophisticated as a nation to find ourselves in this situation. Historically, we have been in this place many times before. While studying the Book of Judges, God's word reminds us of people like Othniel, Ehud, and Shamgar, whom He brought forth to save the people. Every time He would save the people, and it was just a matter of time before they returned to their evil ways. Times like these, we should not shrink back. It is the divine task for all believers in Christ to pass on the light we receive from God. Your light is needed more now than ever before. What will you do with your light?

Ephesians 5:6-17

"Let no one deceive you with empty words, for because of these things the wrath of God comes upon the sons of disobedience. Therefore, do not become partners with them; for at one time you were darkness, but now you are light in the Lord. Walk as children of light (for the fruit of light is found in all that is good and right and true), and try to discern what is pleasing to the Lord. Take no part in the unfruitful works of darkness, but instead expose them. For it is shameful even to speak of the things that they do in secret. But when anything is exposed by the light, it becomes visible, for anything that becomes visible is light. Therefore, it says, 'Awake, O sleeper, and arise from the dead, and Christ will shine on you.' Look carefully then how you walk, not as unwise but as wise, making the best use of the time, because the days are evil. Therefore, do not be foolish, but understand what the will of the Lord is."

☙ Pause and Reflect ☙

It's okay to check off the boxes and manage your schedule—but don't just check off the boxes and not live life. It is perfectly fine to find joy and happiness in the tasks you are called to do for God. Allow yourself to enjoy the blessings and opportunities God gives to you. Let your light shine for Jesus. Think about the areas of your life where you bring about positive change. How did you feel before, during, and after affecting the positive change? Did those changes affect you and your perception with recognizing God's presence in assisting you with tasks? Write about these times and discuss how seeing those opportunities come to fruition impacted your life and the lives of others. Answer the following questions to assist you with uncovering changes you may consider incorporating with future growth opportunities.

1. What is your mindset when you complete tasks or confront obstacles?

2. Do you adopt a positive or negative approach? Take note of what it felt like to approach life positively. Contrast it with having a negative disposition. Which approach works best?

3. Do you allow your God-given light to shine in everything you do?

4. What actions or personal fulfillment can you achieve to make your inner light shine brighter?

18
ஓ ♥ ஓ

God's Favor

As you travel along the path God set specifically for you, He shows and teaches you about Him, yourself, and the tasks He has called you to do for His glory. The walk of my Christian journey hasn't been easy. I would guess yours hasn't been either.

I can remember thinking and simultaneously saying to God, "Why is being a Christian so hard?" He answered right back, "Because you are making it hard." I was in disbelief of the answer—not in disbelief He answered me, but to hear the truth and the reality from God that I was the one making it hard was an unexpected blow to me. I had to look inside myself. I knew God always loved me. There wasn't any doubt in my mind!

However, in my pursuit of growing closer to God and my Savior Jesus Christ, unknowingly, I delayed the development of this spiritual relationship. Why would I even think I was the culprit? After all, I already accepted Jesus as my Lord and Savior. I believed Jesus died for my sins and rose from the dead. I turned from my sins and invited Jesus into my heart and life. I trusted and followed Jesus as my Lord and Savior.

God's favor was, and is, upon me and you. Sadly, in my pursuit, I was overthinking, overanalyzing, and just too inundated with life's circumstances to feel His presence and hear His voice. I was trying too hard to please Him when He already loved me. Even as I overcommitted and wouldn't say no to any request of me, God kept right on loving me through it all.

Jeremiah 1:5

"Before I formed you in the womb, I knew you, and before you were born, I consecrated you; I appointed you a prophet to the nations."

God made you and me. He knows all the qualities we possess, and He knows our faults. He knows all about us. How couldn't He know His creation? But guess what? He still loves us through our transgressions and faults. I was trying to be this perfect person for Christ, even knowing Jesus is the only one who is perfect and worthy to be praised. Not only was I hindering the development of my relationship and maturity in Christ, I was running around doing a bunch of busy work to prove my worthiness.

Romans 8:38-39

"For I am sure that neither death nor life, nor angels nor rulers, nor things present nor things to come, nor powers, nor height nor depth, nor anything else in all creation will be able to separate us from the love of God in Christ Jesus our Lord."

If your walk seems difficult, I implore you to look at your approach. My daughter said to me a few years ago, "Mom, all of the people who are doing the wrong things and who are mean to people seem to have everything, while people like me, who try to live right and do the right things, seem to struggle. So why should we keep being nice to get knocked down by them?" If you wonder the same, just know there will be glory after this. God will turn it around. You have to keep the faith and make the development of your relationship with God through Christ easy, not hard like I did. Pray for God's wisdom, discernment, and guidance as you walk in His favor. Use God's word as a weapon against the tempter and those he uses to tempt you.

I made my walk harder for myself. I made God's requirement of me more difficult than it really is to be a faithful follower of Christ. My maturing faith allowed me to understand that developing a relationship with God through our Lord and Savior Jesus Christ is as easy as putting one foot in front of the other. Your walk of faith can be as easy as walking across a room. You get to determine how difficult it will be based upon your belief system. Yes, there will be obstacles placed before you while you seek to strengthen your relationship with God; it is imperative for you to understand this as you begin or continue your journey. Therefore, do not be surprised when your faith is tested or life appears to fall apart all around you.

I wasn't able to hear Him after praying for answers or seeking a particular directive on a situation. Talk about feeling like you are in the wilderness. This feeling of loneliness is not comfortable at all. The good news is He is with you and is working for your good, even when you are unable to hear or feel Him.

So many times we put limits on when and how God will answer our prayers. He knows what we need before we ask, and sometimes our prayers do not align with what we need in our lives—even when we think we need them. All we need is a little bit of faith and trust in God to work it out for us. As we wait and keep the faith and trust in the Lord, we realize the power of God. God's favor always shows up in our lives on time, not when we demand His favor. It appears when we have done the work. Remember God's word says He will never forsake nor leave us.

The continued effort of seeking Him will lead you to His presence, His peace, and His joy.

☙ Pause and Reflect ☙

Have you approached your relationship with God like I discussed in this chapter? Developing a relationship with God is a lot easier than we allow ourselves to believe. His word and Jesus are clear indications of His love for us.

1. Do you accept Jesus as your Lord and Savior? Do you believe God loves you?

2. Are you willing to walk away from the people or situations that keep your light dim?

3. How much time are you willing to study to learn God's word? How often will you seek Him through prayer and meditating on His word?

4. In what ways have you gained His favor? What routines or practices do you regularly adopt or share with others to better yourself and your community?

19

Perfect Timing

Several weeks before completing this book, I had trouble adhering to the timeline I outlined to finish writing. I arranged a virtual meeting with a friend to discuss the pressure I felt from the delayed completion. During our call, she asked me several questions about how I perceived God's reaction to not completing this book. She began to rapidly fire questions at me, almost giving me no time to answer before firing another question.

My response was always the same. "God will love me no matter when I finish the book" and "He isn't going to stop showing up for me if I don't complete the book." However, I told her I knew the writing of this book was an assignment from God and that it must be completed. It wasn't a matter of when I completed the book; it was simply a matter of fulfilling the assignment He gave me.

She told me Satan, the tempter, was trying to keep me from completing my assignment. We talked about making agreements and signing contracts with a negative spirit. This can happen by simply speaking a word of negativity aloud or having a negative feeling about a particular situation, task, or even yourself. She took me through a series of steps to use the authority given to us by Jesus to renounce those negative thoughts and words, which unknowingly lead to agreements. By the authority given to us by Jesus's resurrection, crucifixion, and ascension, we can break those agreements.

Having no prior exposure to this type of renouncing exercise, I walked through the process and at the end rebuked the spirit and sent it to Jesus Christ for His judgment. We have the authority to send the enemy away. The power, though, is in His name and authority.

After we prayed and ended the meeting, I became even more resolute in my desire to finish this book. God's desire for the completion of this book would not be delayed by the tempter who tried to trap me into a contract and not complete it. People are waiting to read this book. God is trying to reach people with my story to help them along their respective journeys.

As I mentioned earlier, we are in the midst of the COVID-19 virus pandemic and unrest in our society due to the continued racial injustices in this world. The timing of my story isn't late at all. It's right on time! God is never early or late; He is always on time.

I have lived and observed the actions and reactions of all people with the perspective of a biracial child who grew into a woman. It's amazing how as a young, naive child I understood the unequal treatment of individuals based upon their skin color. It wasn't because I was taught about it at home. My mom was afraid to talk about race and race relations because she understood the complexities of her situation. She understood the hatred of those who felt races shouldn't "mix." She understood at any time we could be attacked or killed for her decision to keep and love me as her child, going against what society felt was acceptable. I am unaware of all that she went through as a black female during that specific period of time with a half-white child. Sadly, racial injustice still exists. After all these decades, I hoped that those prejudices would have improved or ended.

Over the years, I heard people say they aren't racist, and they don't understand how racism exists. First, it exists because we are in denial about our individual feelings toward different races of people. Some people can't see beyond this difference. Second, racism continues because we teach our children the very same feelings of denial about racism, and in some cases, we teach our children to be racist through our actions, words, and deeds. We teach hate for others because of the hue of their skin. Third, even when our words are the right ones, our actions reveal our true feelings. We implicitly teach our children that some people are better than others based on the color of their skin. As a child and an adult, I witnessed the feelings of inadequacy forced onto others via the actions and words of both black and white people. Along my life journey, I can't begin to tell you about all the hurt and pain I experienced and saw others experience at the hands of racist people who refused to believe racism exists.

This racial injustice isn't new; it began before I was born. This same racial injustice kept my parents and other couples like them from openly loving someone because of the color of their skin. This injustice didn't allow me to experience having a father present in my home. This same racial injustice allowed white people to make black people feel inferior.

My experiences in life with racism don't lie at the feet of any one ethnic group. I experienced the impact of racism at the hand of both white and black people. This type of racial superiority on either side is not what God expected from us when He created us or when He gave Moses the second greatest commandment to love your neighbor as yourself.

This type of racial tension is happening because we refuse to follow the commands given to us by God. I am currently on my fourth reading of the Bible. Every morning when I read my daily chapter of the Bible, it feels as if I am reading about the state of the world right now. We are a hardheaded people. We have forgotten how God told us to live. There are so many offenses against Him and His word that some of us commit repeatedly. We look down our noses at others if they are different than us. We attack others for their beliefs. We attack others because we perceive them to have accomplished more than we have in our own life. We attack others for desiring to approach life differently than us. This list goes on and on about why we treat some people differently than those we love.

God's word doesn't say love someone if they look like you or love someone because they are a part of a group or clique you want to be a part of; we are called to love everyone. It's amazing how the tempter uses our uniqueness against us to take our souls. The tempter comes to kill, steal, and destroy. **Psalm 31:15-22**

"My times are in your hand; rescue me from the hand of my enemies and from my persecutors! Make your face shine on your servant; save me in your steadfast love! O Lord, let me not be put to shame, for I call upon you; let the wicked be put to shame; let them go silently to Sheol. Let the lying lips be mute, which speak insolently against the righteous in pride and contempt. Oh, how abundant is your goodness, which you have stored up for those who fear you and worked for those who take refuge in you, in the sight of the children of mankind! In the cover of our presence, you hide them from the plots of men; you store them in your shelter from the strife of tongues. Blessed be the Lord, for he has wondrously shown his steadfast love to me when I was in a besieged city. 'I am cut off from your sight.' But you heard the voice of my pleas for mercy when I cried to you for help. Love the Lord, all you His saints! The Lord preserves the faithful but abundantly repays the one who acts in pride. Be strong and let your heart take courage, all you who wait for the Lord!"

The sin of prejudice leads to many other sins from a purely emotional perspective. Most of us have prejudices, whether taught to us or developed from our own experiences. The good news is God loved us so much that He sent us His one and only Son Jesus Christ to die for our sins. What will you do with the love shown to you by God?

What will you do with the blood shed by our Savior for you? Are you going to allow prejudices to keep you from spending eternity with our Savior Jesus Christ?

Obstacles all around us threaten our ability to be the best versions of who we are created to be for God's glory; take His word with you everywhere you go to fight that which threatens the real prize of your life—your relationship with the Lord. Remember, God's timing is perfect, and it's never too late to press toward the mark of service and redemption.

☙ Pause and Reflect ☙

Search your heart, mind, and soul for situations where you have felt like you were better than someone or more experienced than someone chosen over you for a particular task or situation for any of the reasons mentioned above. You may have additional reasons that are unique to you. Explore the thoughts you think God has about your feelings of superiority. Do you think you embody the thoughts, ideas, and fortitude necessary to keep His commandment to love thy neighbor as you love yourself?

1. Have you experienced a time when you felt you were better than others? What gave you that feeling of superiority? Do you believe you are superior because of your race?

2. Has your feeling of superiority caused pain or hurt for someone else? What benefits did you receive from this perceived superiority?

3. Are your feelings of superiority indicative of what God calls us to do—love your neighbor as you love yourself?

4. Are you able to change your perspective of those who are of a different race or ethnicity? How could you positively impact someone of a different race or ethnicity?

20
❧ ♥ ❧

Power

I am sure you have endured some hurtful experiences at the hands of other people's unawareness of their actions and how they impact others; most people are usually focused on their happiness, while not considering how their actions or words affect other people. You may have also endured some hurtful feelings from the intentional actions of someone deliberately causing you harm and pain. It is my belief that those people will reap what they have sown. They may have won on the surface, but God's word says otherwise.

I remember sitting in my car at a stoplight the summer of my sophomore year in college. Another car with two young white men pulled up beside me. They had their window rolled down, and so did I. One of the guys told his friend how pretty I was, and he had never seen anyone with my complexion.

The other guy blurted, "Oh, she's a mulatto." The first guy didn't know the term "mulatto." As the light turned green and I started to drive away, I could hear the second guy begin to explain what it meant. I remember, in that moment, feeling a very quick sense of fear for my safety. I checked my rearview mirror several times to make sure they weren't following me as I turned onto the highway.

This particular experience showcases someone taught about racism and someone who wasn't taught about racism. The second guy knew I was the product of black and white parents. The first guy was oblivious to the facts of my conception. Over the years, I wondered how the rest of the conversation between the two guys went that day. While I will never know, I truly hope both of them had an opportunity to interact with a "mulatto" at some point in their life and took the time to get to know the person, instead of judging them based upon the color of their skin.

Looking back over my life, I clearly see I was created and born for specific reasons. Over and over again, I have seen the ugly faces of racism from all types of people. This specific retribution never made any logical sense to me. To have an individual dislike me because of the color of my skin is just unconscionable. While I loved my parents and admire them for the strength and resolve they represented, I couldn't choose my parents, and neither could you. God knew who he wanted us born to and how He wanted us to serve Him before we were born.

Throughout my life, I was able to overcome the ugliness of the very injustices we experience today at the hands of multiple ethnic groups. You have the power to choose not to take negative experiences personally. Racism, like other forms of discrimination, comes from the refusal to understand that we were all created by God. We weren't allowed to ask God for the parents we wanted or for our skin color to be what we wanted, for we did not have any say in His creation! It was totally out of our hands. He chose the color of our skin.

The bigoted encounters and experiences as a biracial person are certainly unpleasant. Experiencing the hatred of others because they aren't accepting of others' differences has to be viewed from a lens of love. I am evidence and not a coincidence of God's love. He knew before He created you or me the power we would need to endure such behavior at the hands of individuals who choose to believe hatred of others is acceptable. There is never justification to attack anyone, but the difference in skin color is not a reason to treat others differently or make them feel insufficient as a person.

I am so glad that I knew at a very young age not to buy any of their wolf tickets. The misguided hatred I endured made me stronger and resolute in my desire to succeed. All this time, God has been developing His power in me. He created the same power in you as well! Being a biracial individual was not the end of my story; it was the beginning. I have had to deal with the offenses of others because of the color of my skin my entire life. I liken it to the offenses David dealt with because he was young and small in stature, and so many thought he was just a boy. He couldn't possibly defeat a giant. Thanks be to God, David realized who he was! He knew he didn't create himself; God created him in His own image, just like He created you and me. David also recognized God delivered him from the lion and the bear. He remembered what God had done for him before and knew without a shadow of a doubt God would be with him and deliver him from Goliath. David went against Goliath in the name of the Lord. David knew the battle was the Lord's, and he knew God would give Goliath over into his hands.

What is your Goliath? Look back over your life at the things God has brought you through and move forward to conquer your Goliath. God has done so much for me over my lifetime that I can only scratch the surface if I tried to tell you about them all. I had to learn all the battles I faced were not mine; they were the Lord's. I can now rest assured that when I face big or small challenges, God will see me through it all. ***Psalm 147:5***

"Great is our Lord, and abundant in power; his understanding is beyond measure."

I learned not to sweat the small stuff. Yes, someone's opinion about who I am because of my skin color is small stuff! You see, I am more than a biracial woman. I am who God says I am! He is the author and the finisher, and He created me for His glory. Don't allow others' feelings toward you to keep you stuck in places and spaces without

God. You must realize the power within yourself and move past the offense others wish to impart upon you with the hopes of keeping you from reaching your destiny.

Turn the ugliness of such people into motivation to help you become the person you were created to become. God is looking for the better version of you! When you seek to become that individual, the offenses, hatred, or bigotry thrown at you will not matter—because the intended destruction will not materialize.

Recently, my husband was preparing for a speaking engagement, and we talked about how he would accomplish the task. While discussing the situation, I told him to take the power of God with him, and he would be victorious. I spoke those words with so much conviction in God. I remember thinking, *Where did such conviction come from?* The conviction came from many years of building a relationship with God and Jesus. It came from the faith I have in God to finish the great works He has begun.

The Lord knows I endured enough testimony-building challenges that I could write several books and give anyone doubting God's grace and mercy enough evidence to trust His promises learned from my story. Those challenges made me strong; those challenges made me who I am today. The road traveled hasn't been easy, but my journey allowed me to trust in the Lord and take the power of God wherever I go. You will face many hurdles along your journey, but if you remember the power you have in God through our Lord and Savior Jesus Christ, they will be made easier. You can then accept both pleasant and unpleasant elements of the future that you may face along your journey.

My charge to you is not to question how or why God does what He does in our lives. Usually, God doesn't proceed the way we think He will when helping His children. God's timing is perfect. We are called to trust God and keep the faith, especially when you don't understand His plan. We must trust Him to work it out for us, even when we cannot feel His presence or see opportunity moving in our direction. Hold on to God's promises, even when life isn't going as you planned. ***Isaiah 54:4***

> *"Fear not, for you will not be ashamed; be not confounded, for you will not be disgraced; for you will forget the shame of your youth, and the reproach of your widowhood you will remember no more."*

There are so many situations placed before us every moment of a given day that try to knock us off of God's plan for our lives. I speak from experience; there are times when it is a moment-by-moment battle to remember the power we have inside of us. ***1 John 4:1-6***

> *"Beloved, do not believe every spirit, but test the spirits to see whether they are from God, for many false prophets have gone out into the world. By this you know the Spirit of God: every spirit that confesses that Jesus Christ has come in the flesh is from God, and every spirit that does not confess Jesus is not from God. This is the spirit of the antichrist, which you heard was coming and now is in the world already. Little children, you are from God and have overcome them, for He who is in you is greater than he who is in the world. They are from the world; therefore they speak from the world, and the world listens to them. We are from God. Whoever knows God listens to us; whoever is not from God does not listen to us. By this we know the Spirit of truth and the spirit of error."*

Always remember the power you carry with you as a child of God. Keep your eyes on Him as you live your life, trusting, knowing, and believing without a shadow of a doubt that greater is in you than he who is in the world. God has so many plans for each one of us. It is during those times when God seems so far away that we must realize He is with us the entire time.

His hand of protection, provision, and power is available to all who believe His word and the covenant He made with Abraham, Isaac, and Jacob. Keep pressing forward with God on your side, and you will be unstoppable in your pursuits! God's power is given only by Him. Just like the peace and joy He gives to those of us who believe, it cannot be taken away from you by anyone else. Stand firm on God's word and refuse to give the gifts given to you by God away to others. Some people don't want to see you happy or don't want to see you walk in the destiny God has for you; they want to see discord and distress in your life. You have the power of God to tell them all they are liars and that you walk in the plans God has for you. Trust God in every area of your life and take only those who are with you, not against you.

If you are surrounded by takers and those who won't make themselves available to you to celebrate you and your accomplishments and maintain the chaos in your life—and for that matter their lives—you should kindly step away from them. Their actions and disposition determine if you should allow someone to hold lifetime space in your life. Their actions determine if you continue to grow with them or without them. You can't determine what type of person an individual may be, but you can refuse to continue to let them foster chaos in your life.

When you continue to let takers be a part of your life, you are unable to see God's power waiting to operate in your life. It's not hard or difficult to develop a relationship with our creator. God made us, and He wants us to have an intimate relationship with Him. What are you waiting for? Everything you experience is worth gaining God's power to confidently apply in every situation of your life. Of all of my accomplishments, I am most proud of realizing this because of the power I was given by God through Jesus Christ.

You, too, have this very same power. But will you do the work to uncover the person God created you to be in Jesus? Will you walk away from people and places who prevent you from becoming the person who possesses the power of God? This, just like everything in your life, is your responsibility. I desire to carry God's power with me every single day.

To uncover the power, first, you must admit your relationship with God needs some work. Do you read and study the scripture? Do you pray and make petitions to God for others, your family, and yourself? Do you spend time in God's presence? Do you talk with other believers about God's promise? Do you continue to interact with nonbelievers who dump their baggage onto you because you allow them to do so? You must be deliberate about the relationship you have with God, and you must develop the person God created you to be to recognize the power of God within you. I challenge you from this day forward to be deliberate in every area of your life and watch God's power show up on your behalf in all areas of your life. ***Ephesians 5:15-17***

"Be very careful, then, how you live—not as unwise but as wise, making the most of every opportunity, because the days are evil. Therefore do not be foolish, but understand what the Lord's will is."

In writing this book, I began to appreciate the power of God within me. I initially doubted my ability to write this book, but through it all, God allowed me to realize the power I have from within to fulfill the assignments He placed me on this earth to complete for His glory. God is good! He wants you to experience freedom—freedom not to feel the bondage others purposefully pass on to you, as well as the bondage from those who unknowingly burden you with their negative feelings, outlooks, and expectations when they are merely trying to survive themselves. If you still have doubts about this God-given power, I say step out on faith. What do you have to lose? You may ask, "What do I have to gain?" God's power is what you have to gain!

❧ Pause and Reflect ☙

Reflect on times in your life where you needed to take the power of God with you to complete an assignment. When feelings of inadequacy begin to creep into a situation you are involved with, it's important to remember God is with us, and He provides His power for us to see things to completion.

1. Did you have faith that God would help you through certain issues? Did you try to fix it alone?

2. What might have been a different outcome if you had the power of God with you?

3. What does it mean to take the power of God with you? What is your perception of God's power?

4. Will you share the good news about the power of God?

21

Conviction

Recognizing the power within ourselves allows us to overcome the obstacles we face during our lifetime. Developing awareness of the source of our strength source gives us the chance to move forward, even when life is off-track and we are unable to see our life's potential.

Certain situations or people can impede our ability to move beyond our current challenge or milestone. I call these the "showstoppers." They might stop you dead in your tracks, not allowing you to move forward until you complete the necessary self-reflection to acknowledge what may hold you back if left unattended. The other possibility is you move forward thinking all your bases are covered and everything is just fine—while those underlying issues remain undiscussed or dormant in your mind, waiting to cause havoc when all appears to be going well.

Simple awareness of the possible hindrances will allow you to move forward with conviction because you consciously allowed yourself to discover the roadblocks, instead of burying them in the sand to rear their ugly heads later, causing you to question the promises and the love of God. While Satan seeks to kill, steal, and destroy, your preparation allows you to fall back on God's love, grace, and mercy, which give you the strength to weather any storm.

A relationship with God requires obedience. Your obedience to God allows you to recognize God's voice and discern when He guides you. Your obedience allows you to be blessed by God because you trust Him, His Holy Spirit, and His Word to reign in your life—with the faith He will be true to His word. We don't have to control every single facet of our lives when we focus on the Lord, trusting He will keep His promises.

When God started trusting me with a little, he was preparing me to be trusted with a lot. The opportunities and situations all grew incrementally in size, scope, and responsibility over my life. Sometimes, I was totally aware of where God was leading me, and other times, I didn't have a clue about His direction. I didn't understand why I had to experience and endure some of the painful situations this world offered me. I merely relied on my God-given resolve to keep pressing toward the mark.

Psalm 118:24

"This is the day that the Lord has made; let us rejoice and be glad in it."

I made the decision to trust God. When will you decide in your mind that "this is the day?" When we make the decision to trust in God and keep the faith no matter what comes our way, every day is "the day." There are new mercies granted every single day. You have to choose how you will use those new mercies. Will you actively pursue the people and situations God continues to prepare for you, or will you bury the abilities He gives to recognize those mercies?

The choice is yours. This is the day to open yourself to the opportunities that await you. This is the day to trust in the Lord to see you through it all: the good, the bad, and the ugly. How will you persevere through "this day?" Will you choose to be an example for all to see, or will you continue to search for the example in someone else? God has grown you and me through a lot of little experiences and a lot of other people ultimately trying to bring us to the big plans He has for all who are obedient and trust Him. ***Psalm 31:19-20***

> *"Oh, how abundant is your goodness, which you have stored up for those who fear you and worked for those who take refuge in you, in the sight of the children of mankind! In the cover of your presence, you hide them from the plots of men; you store them in your shelter from the strife of tongues."*

Every day of your life is a new opportunity to be the best you can be in every area of your life. Make the decision to receive the new mercies available to you! This mercy doesn't mean everything we experience going forward will be a positive situation. On the contrary, there will be people and situations placed before you that challenge your remembrance of God's word. They will try to make you doubt yourself, your abilities, and God. As you encounter these types of experiences, it is important you trust in the Lord.

We must become resolute in our trust in God to help us through the temptations we face in life. Will you allow the short-term success you achieve through evil and wrongdoing entice you to succumb to a world of the same? Think about what your eternity looks like because of your actions or lack thereof. Reevaluate whose child you are and which path you are called to take. God calls all of us to greater. Decide "this day" that you will answer the call of God and watch Him take you beyond your greatest expectations.

☙ Pause and Reflect ❧

We are called to approach situations with a conviction and expectation that God is with us. Inviting Him into your presence and your life allows you to move forward in boldness. This boldness allows you to move forward with an expectation of covering. Oftentimes, life will not progress as originally planned or the way you believed it would happen. However, my faith and conviction ensure I am not alone as I move forward. Have you grown spiritually?

1. How can you be more obedient to God?

2. Will you allow conflict, self-doubt, or the act of oppression by others to keep you from being obedient to God?

3. What can you do each day to move toward the plans God has prepared for you? Call on God to help you through!

22

Victory

Victory is a time when all the hard work and dedication pays off, and the end result yields a positive influence. We must all understand these provisions are made because of the great love He has for us. God makes a way out of none. He opens doors for us to continue our journey, and He closes those or keeps shut the doors not meant for us to walk through.

Our God is great! He loves us enough not to leave us in situations without growth. We should always strive to grow while we move toward the mark. ***Isaiah 45:1-3***

> *"Thus says the Lord to his anointed, to Cyrus, whose right hand I have grasped, to subdue the nations before him and to loose the belts of kings, to open doors before him that gates may not be closed; I will go before you and level the exalted places, I will break in pieces the doors of bronze and cut through the bars of iron, I will give you the treasures of darkness and the hoards in secret places, that you may know that it is I, the Lord, the God of Israel, who call you by your name."*

God's love has aided many victories in my life. His love for me allowed me to grow and develop in so many ways beyond my imagination. His love for me allows me to be a daughter, a wife, a mother, an employee, an employer, a friend, a leader, a teacher, a deacon, and a stock-market operator. God prepared me for all these roles individually, which collectively make up who I am as a total person.

Someone asked me when I was a high school student what I wanted to do in life. The response I gave is one that still holds true today: "I want to be a success!" Success has taken on different outcomes in every phase of my journey. I experienced peaks and valleys, sunshine and rain, but through it all, God never left my side! I am so grateful God didn't give up on me. I am victorious, and you are victorious because of God's favor. *2 Corinthians 2:14-17*

> *"But thanks be to God, who in Christ always leads us in triumphal procession, and through us spreads the fragrance of the knowledge of him everywhere. For we are the aroma of Christ to God among those who are being saved and among those who are perishing, to one a fragrance from death to death, to the other a fragrance from life to life. Who is sufficient for these things? For we are not, like so many, peddlers of God's word, but as men of sincerity, as commissioned by God, in the sight of God we speak in Christ."*

God ultimately wanted me to share my story, but not to center it around me, as I originally envisioned. The true story is and always will be about God, Jesus, and the Holy Spirit. It's about God's love, grace, and mercy. Tell someone your story. Tell them how God has never left you nor forsaken you. Be the example of God's victory and share His light everywhere you go.

❧ Pause and Reflect ❧

There are so many moments where we count our victories as our own. Once we pass through those valley moments, we attribute the success to how great we are and forget God was there carrying us through to the other side of completion. As you reflect over what God allowed you to achieve, are you able to identify where his assistance began and where it ended? Thinking back on those accomplishments, do you remember giving God praise for allowing you to see it through? Did you give Him praise for your victories? If you didn't, now is a great time to capture them and give God praise for that which He worked for your good and those gifts you were presented with that caused growth in your life.

1. Since reading this book and journaling in these moments of reflection, has your outlook and perspective changed when dealing with people, issues, or concerns?

2. Do you find yourself seeking God's guidance before you make decisions?

3. Do you find yourself talking with God before you talk with a friend or coworker when faced with a decision?

4. Has your relationship with God and Jesus strengthened since reading this book?

23

Reflection

As I remember the morning God gave me the assignment to write this book, I reflect on the content I thought I would cover. I remember thinking I must tell my story—I was born of a biracial couple at a time when it was unacceptable to form a relationship with someone of the opposite race. I jotted notes about my calling to write this book for those who struggle to fit comfortably inside any ethnic group because of their multiracial existence.

I wanted to move full speed ahead and talk about all my hurtful experiences at the hands of individuals who were insensitive to my feelings as a person. I wanted to write a book to save the little mixed-race girls and boys from experiencing this same pain growing up. I wanted to tell them how beautiful, smart, and intelligent they were, regardless of the treatment they would receive at the hands of people who chose hatred over love.

Ultimately, this story wasn't told as I originally envisioned. God wanted me to talk about injustices and obstacles. Someone needed to hear the details of my story to understand that their differences aren't weaknesses—they are strengths colored in a different cloth. For me to share the details of my story, I also had to tell the story of God's love. After all, it all begins with Him! He loves us so much that He sent us His one and only begotten Son, Jesus Christ, who suffered at the hands of people who didn't believe He was the Son of God. Those same people sought to kill him. Those people mocked him, nailed Him to a cross, pierced His side, and put a crown of thorns on His head. The very same people were ignorant to the power Jesus possessed and still possesses. How could they not know who they were torturing?

Jesus got down off that cross and descended and came back to walk among His people before He ascended into Heaven, where He sits on the right side of God Almighty. He is the one who left His Holy Spirit, which lives and dwells in you and me. ***1 John 4:4-6***

"Little children, you are from God and have overcome them, for He who is in you is greater than he who is in the world. They are from the world; therefore, they speak from the world, and the world listens to them. We are from God. Whoever knows God listens to us. By this we know the spirit of truth and the spirit of falsehoods."

They chose not to know. They chose to ignore what was right in front of their eyes. They saw the signs and wonders performed by Jesus, and they still refused to acknowledge Him. Sadly, those same types of individuals choose to walk in hatred, bitterness, and jealousy while inflicting the same injustices imposed upon Jesus onto God's people.
1 John 4:7-13

"Beloved, let us love one another, for love is from God, and whoever loves has been born of God and knows God. Anyone who does not love does not know God, because God is love. In this the love of God was made manifest among us, that God sent His one and only Son into the world, so that we might live through Him. In this is love, not that we have loved God, but that He loved us and sent his Son to be the propitiation for our sins. Beloved, if God so loved us, we also ought to love one another. No one has ever seen God; if we love one another,

REFLECTION

God abides in us, and his love is perfected in us. By this we know that we abide in Him and He in us because He has given us of His Spirit."

My story as a biracial person is intertwined with the very essence of love—God's love! He knew exactly who He was creating when He made you and me. He created me against the norm of society's expectations. He created individuals like me ethnically, even when He knew we wouldn't fit in any one situation nicely and neatly. He created us with such power, if we choose to learn of His love, grace, and mercy.

My story entails the love of two unsuspecting people from two different backgrounds and ethnicities chosen for my conception. God chose my mother and my father, who loved me regardless of the looks, stares, jeers, comments, and heartache they received because they were God's chosen vessels for my creation.

Through writing this book, I grew to understand the magnitude of my existence. It is with great admiration of the miracles of God that I grew to learn, understand, realize, and accept all that God orchestrated to bring me forth. This book allowed me to finally put some of the pieces of the puzzle in perspective. I hope you experienced some of the same moments of clarity as you read this book and wrote in your journal. God has plans for you! He has prepared you and me for such a time as this.

So many times, in life, we allow other people and different circumstances to decide our destiny and influence our self-worth without realizing we bought into their negative narratives of who we are and what we don't bring to the table. We experience enough negativity at the hands of others that, somehow, we begin to accept and give in to their thought processes.

Break those negative thoughts you have unknowingly made to be mediocre! You owe it to yourself to move beyond the negativity and realize the fullness of God's love, grace, and mercy. Not only do you owe it to yourself, but you owe it all to God, who created you for His glory. The greatness you look for is found in Him! He wants you to say "yes" to the plans that He created just for you.

Accepting my biracial identity allowed me to accept the uniqueness of all God's children, appreciate the differences, and respect His creations. I don't hold any preconceived ideas about any individual. I allow them to show me who they are through their actions, works, and deeds. Then I believe them based upon the picture they paint of their heart. Learn to trust your intuition; when we align ourselves with God, He reveals His will and gives us peace surrounding people and situations we encounter. He wants us to continually seek a relationship with Him and His people.

Life isn't always as it seems. Seek individuals who see the value of getting to know you and others for who they are, not those who assume someone's ability based on the color of their skin or appearance. When we allow ourselves to be close-minded when interacting with different people, we miss out on the gifts God gave to all of His children. We must actively seek God to realize those gifts.

My challenge to you is to be the best God created you to be as an individual. Get to know and surround yourself with other individuals who share this challenge and move forward to cause a change in someone's life. Don't place a limit on the expectations of God's calling on your life. God wants you to walk into your destiny! The Spirit of the Living God is available and waiting for His children to walk with Him! The choice is yours. What will you do?

I have decided to continue my walk with God fully accepting that I am evidence, not a coincidence, of God's love!

www.ingramcontent.com/pod-product-compliance
Lightning Source LLC
LaVergne TN
LVHW010343070526
838199LV00065B/5780